Disaster Planning Made Easy

Marty Augustine

"The past created our present. Our plans create the future."

Marty Augustine

Disaster Planning Made Easy

Introduction

A disaster can happen anywhere, at any time...
Are you prepared?

Many people are unaware of the many dangers that lurk in our everyday lives. Life threatening hazards are all around us.

You will most likely encounter a disaster or hazardous situation at some time in your life. No one is immune.

It's not a matter of if a disaster will strike, but when...

Some disasters may offer advance warning, others may strike without warning. How you prepare may be the difference between life and death. The purpose of this book is to provide you with the basic concepts of emergency preparedness.

Everyone, both young and old, should be ready for a harmful incident. Admitting and accepting that you could become a victim is the first step in preparedness. This book will guide you through the complex world of disasters. The responsibility of emergency planning and preparedness is shared by all.

This book provides information on things you can do to lessen the inconvenience, should a disaster occur. When something does happen, you'll be mentally and physically prepared for whatever comes your way.

Chapter 1

Basics of Emergency Planning

Creating an Emergency Plan

Creating an emergency plan will help you deal with a disaster in a less stressful manner. The old saying of "practice makes perfect" holds true here. Plan well and your emergency situation will be better controlled.

Some disasters may be small, simply causing minor inconvenience. Others may be large and cause widespread destruction. Always hope for the best, but prepare for the worst case scenario.

The first thing to do before a disaster is to learn what types of threats you could potentially be exposed to. This is called a hazard analysis. The purpose of a hazard analysis is to assess your risks and identify ways of controlling or eliminating them.

By doing this, you can focus on hazards that are most likely to occur in your area. For example, if you live in Minnesota, your chance of being impacted by a hurricane is far less than if you live in Florida. Or, your chance of encountering a blizzard is less in south Texas, than in Maine. It's not to say that the event could not occur, but it is less probable.

Preparing for all types of hazards is important, but planning for what is most likely to impact you is best.

You can learn more about specific threats in your area by contacting your local Red Cross chapter or your local emergency management office. Police and fire departments are also excellent resources for information.

Develop your plan well ahead of time.

Planning will identify problems or concerns that need to be corrected. Planning also brings out many questions that should be addressed before a disaster is upon you.

When a disaster strikes, you may not be with your family or you may not even be at home.

What if you can't get to your kids?

What if you're stuck at work?

Where will you go if you must evacuate?

What if you were stranded in your home?

It's important to take these things into consideration when planning. What would you do if a disaster struck today?

Will your family know what to do if you're not there? Think of ways to lessen the effects of disaster in your life. After you create your plan, be sure to share it with your family.

Practice your plans regularly and make sure *everyone* involved understands them fully. Periodically review your plans and revise them if needed.

Constantly play the "what if" game. Imagine scenarios in your mind and think about how you'd react to them. Watch the nightly news and think about how well you'd be prepared if the news story you watch happened in your area.

As you read through his book, hopefully many of your hard to ask questions will find solutions.

Emergency Preparedness Cycle

The concept of emergency planning is based on the four basic principles of disaster management: Mitigation, Preparedness, Response and Recovery.

Although the four phases of emergency management are four distinct categories, they are a continuous circle. After the recovery phase, the mitigation phase starts again. Each phase compliments the next. The planning circle can begin at any phase.

The 4 phases are applicable to any disaster or emergency situation at home or at work.

Mitigation

This is the act of making an effort to reduce the impact of hazards. Simply put, it is preventing problems before they happen.

For government agencies, mitigation is accomplished through the use of methods such building codes and construction procedures.

Actions such as building a stronger home to withstand an earthquake, or building structures high above flood zones can minimize problems if a disaster strikes.

Mitigation reduces the probability of injury or physical damage resulting from a potential disaster.

Preparedness

This is the act of people actually preparing for a hazard. Preparedness ensures you will be ready to respond to and handle a disaster.

Making sure you have an emergency kit, having adequate supplies and knowing what to do if emergency services are not available are all acts of preparedness.

This practices the idea of being *proactive* rather than *reactive*.

Response

These are the actions taken to respond to an actual emergency or disaster. Response would include fire fighters responding to fires, medical personnel treating the injured and police securing danger areas.

Recovery

The goal of recovery is to return your life and community back to the pre-disaster condition. Restoring essential services, fixing roads and bridges and rebuilding homes and lives occur in this phase.

Important Planning Tips for the Home

You should develop an escape plan for your home in case you need to get out during an emergency. Plan an emergency exit in each room of your home. Always have a back-up exit plan as your primary exit may be blocked.

If you are in a multi-level home, have a plan for upper level escapes. This may include an emergency ladder or other rescue device. In apartment buildings, know the location of designated emergency exits or safe areas.

Designate a meeting point outside your home. Determine a safe spot to re-group and be sure everyone with you knows where to go.

You should also have a second, back up meeting spot somewhere away from your home, in case the first location is not accessible.

Designate a local contact and a third party contact out of state. If someone is out of the disaster area, all parties can check in if they become separated during the incident.

Make sure everyone knows who the contact is, and the telephone number. Keep the emergency numbers in a wallet or backpack.

Remember, disasters may occur while you are away from home. When visiting hotels or other buildings, always know the location of your escape routes and safe rooms (emergency shelters). If in a high rise building, use a stairway to escape. Do not use elevators as you could become trapped.

Every home should have at least one fire extinguisher. Having more than one is even better. Know where your fire extinguisher is and be sure everyone else knows. Make sure everyone in your home knows how to use it. Local fire departments sometimes offer training on the proper use of extinguishers.

Keep one in the kitchen, and if possible, keep one in your garage, basement and car. Read the instructions prior to use to understand how it should be used, as there are various types of fires. Some experts even recommend keeping one in your bedroom.

The most common and best extinguisher to have in your home is an "A,B,C" type (5lb). This is a multi-purpose extinguisher that can be used on a variety of fires. Read the label on the extinguisher to identify the type and intended use.

Be sure the extinguisher is "charged" and in good condition.

A "charged" unit means it ready for use. Every extinguisher should have a gauge on it. The gauge will show a red and green section with an arrow. A good working unit should have the arrow pointing in the green. If the gauge reads red, replace the extinguisher.

Fire extinguishers should only be used on small fires. In the event of a large fire, get everyone out immediately and call 9-1-1 from outside your home. Do not go back inside to retrieve belongings.

Become familiar with your home and know how to shut off your utilities. You should know how to use the water valve, electrical box and gas shut off.

If your gas is turned off, it should only be turned back on by a trained professional. If you are not sure how to use your utilities, ask your neighbors, or a handyman.

It's simple to learn, and useful knowledge to have. If you need to evacuate your home, it is best shut off your utilities before leaving.

Make copies of your identification cards, credit cards, insurance policies and birth certificates. Keep your important documents in a portable flame resistant and water proof container.

Keep your originals or copies in a ready pack that you can with you if need to leave your home in a hurry. Don't forget to include these items for your family members also.

Create an inventory of personal possessions. Document the serial numbers and model numbers of valuable items if possible. Photographs or video recordings of your property are also great ideas.

Keep these protected along with your other important documents.

Animals / Pets

Don't forget to plan ahead for the care of your pets. Pets are often considered to be members of the family. You should always have an emergency plan in place to ensure the safety and care of your pets in the event of a disaster.

If you need to be evacuated, your pets may not be able to go with you. With the exception of service animals, pets are not typically permitted in emergency shelters as they could affect the health and safety of humans.

Search for local hotels and motels that allow pets ahead of time, if you should need a place to stay.

Or, find where pet boarding facilities are located. Be sure to research locations outside of your local area should local facilities be closed or inaccessible.

If you must leave your pets behind as a last resort, leave them with a supply of food and water that should last 3 days as well as adequate shelter for weather conditions.

Be sure your pet has proper ID and up-to-date vaccination records. Keep copies of these records with your personal records.

It's also a good idea to keep a current picture of you with your pet, should you become separated if it gets lost.

Keep a leash and collar on hand as well as any specialty items such as medications, toys, muzzles, etc.

Large Animals

If you have large animals such as horses, cattle, sheep, goats, or pigs on your property, be sure to develop an emergency plan for them before a disaster.

Ensure all animals have some form of identification, evacuate animals whenever possible and always have a back-up plan in case your evacuation route is not accessible.

Follow only the evacuation routes advised by authorities.

Be sure to have the appropriate vehicles needed for transporting and supporting animals available as well as having experienced handlers and drivers ready to assist.

Ensure your final destination will have food, water, veterinary care, and handling equipment. If evacuation is not possible, animal owners must decide whether to move large animals to shelter or turn them outside.

It is best to allow animals a chance to become accustomed to vehicular travel so they are less frightened and easier to move. This should be done before an emergency situation occurs.

Schools

Does your school practice emergency drills for a variety of disaster scenarios? At the very least, they should practice fire drills.

Many schools are now required to practice intruder drills (for active shooters) and severe weather drills where things like tornadoes or earthquakes are a threat.

Find out if school employees are trained on emergency response procedures. If they are not, encourage them to seek training.

If a school must shelter in place, you may not be permitted to pick up your children. The doors will most likely be locked during an incident as a precaution to keep your children safe.

Ask if your local school keeps a supply of food, water, blankets and other emergency supplies should students not be able to leave in case of a disaster.

Find out how your local school communicates with families during emergency situations. Make sure your school has current emergency contact information on file for you.

Always have a backup contact in case you are not available.

Be sure to also designate a family member or friend who can pick up your child if you are unable to. Make sure the school knows who this person is. Also be sure to notify the school of any special needs your child may have.

Get involved during drills to ensure understanding of policies and procedures. If you have questions or suggestions about emergency planning, feel free to contact administrators.

Work

Does your employer practice emergency drills? If a disaster struck while you were at work, would you be prepared? Your workplace should have plans in place for an emergency.

Every building should have an evacuation or safety plan. All employees should be aware of the plan and everyone should participate in emergency drills.

Think about what would happen if you were not allowed to leave work. Would you have adequate supplies?

Does your workplace have an emergency supply kit?

Business owners and managers should learn about emergency planning processes in order to ensure the safety of employees in the workplace. All of the home planning tips can also be applied to the workplace as they are basically the same.

Businesses should appoint a safety representative to assist with emergency planning. Business owners have the responsibility of creating a safe workplace for employees and customers.

Business Continuity

Many businesses fail to properly plan for disasters. A major event could cause serious disruptions for businesses that are not prepared.

Whether you operate a home office, or a large company, the plans should be the same. Buildings could become damaged and rendered unusable.

Critical equipment may be lost or damaged. Important records and files could be destroyed or lost. Employees may not be able to make it in to work because of hazard related issues.

Evaluate your risks and take precautions before a disaster strikes.

If your business plans to operate during and after a disaster, it is important to have a contingency plan in place.

Do you have back up power sources if the public utilities go down?

If your business utilizes equipment that relies on electricity, be sure to have an appropriate power generator and fuel to support operations.

If your primary business location is not able to be used, plan for an alternate operating location ahead of time.

The most important thing for businesses to consider is having a backup for critical systems and documents.

Do not store all of your important files in one location.

Have copies of important documents and store them in a secure location. Things such as payroll, customer order information, inventory and other operational documents should be stored on portable hard drives, internet based storage or at satellite locations.

If you need to evacuate or close your business, you can bring the portable storage with you.

Communication

It is important to let your employees and customers know the status of your business. If you have a website, information can be published online.

For employees, create a phone list or phone tree. Maintain contacts with media outlets such as television stations, radio or newspapers to send out press releases regarding the operating status of your business.

If employees are not able to make it to work, could your business continue to operate? Employees should be cross trained prior to a disaster.

Having knowledge of the duties of other employees can make things run smoother. Be sure employees know what may be expected of them if staffing became an issue. If employees know how to handle other positions, your business can continue to operate with minimum staffing.

Managers can also consider having employees work from home if it is appropriate for your business. Sickness is a major cause of lost revenue. Staffing can become a major issue during times of disease pandemic.

Contagious disease can cripple even the largest of operations. Businesses should limit the exposure of sick employees.

Sick employees should stay home if possible. Encourage the use of hand sanitizers and hand washing to limit the spread of germs in the workplace.

Other Planning Considerations

Become familiar with warnings. Discuss with your family what they should do if alerted. Discuss with your family what they would do if you were not at home when a disaster happens.

Also discuss different threats and warnings with your children. Be sure to practice emergency drills with your family. This can ease fear and make the situation less stressful during an actual event. Be sure to act when an alert is made.

Keep recent photos of your family members and pets. You can provide a photo to authorities if anyone should become lost in a disaster.

Take a course to learn basic first aid and CPR. Include your children in the training. These trainings are offered by the American Red Cross and American Heart Association as well as other organizations. Official certification by the American Red Cross provides legal protection for those giving first aid under the "Good Samaritan" law.

The courses are usually low cost and can save lives.

Always wear a medical alert bracelet if you have special health concerns. Persons with special needs such as the disabled or elderly should prepare with extra care.

If you know of anyone with special needs, be sure that you know where they are during an incident. Be sure to check on them in an emergency as they may not see or hear warnings.

Allow extra time in dealing with their needs. Disabilities may hinder evacuation or rescue. If you think you might require assistance in an emergency, discuss your disability with relatives, friends, or co-workers. Ask for their help if needed.

Many public safety agencies keep registers of people with disabilities. This aids in locating those with disabilities during a disaster or emergency response.

Contact your local fire department or emergency management office for more information.

Post emergency numbers near telephones. Teach children how and when to use 911 to summon emergency services.

You should also consider purchasing insurance for your home and belongings before a disaster strikes. Home owners insurance can protect you from financial disaster if your home and property are damaged.

If you rent or lease your home or an apartment, consider renters insurance. These policies can protect your personal belongings.

Flood insurance is critical if you live in flood prone areas, but it is not usually included as a part of standard insurance policies. Consult an insurance agent for more information regarding these policies.

We plan so we can minimize the risk of property damage, injury or death. Don't wait until something happens to find out you are not prepared. Take some time to think your individual needs and the needs of your family.

Think about what types of threats you may encounter. Always ask yourself "what if" something happened. This will help you develop a better plan.

CHAPTER 2

Building an Emergency Kit

If a disaster should occur, you may not have access to grocery stores or other needs. Businesses may be closed or damaged. Roads may not be passable. You may be stranded at home or another location for an extended period of time.

It is because of this that we must be prepared to sustain ourselves for an extended period of time. Your emergency kit should contain water, food, first aid supplies and other items that will allow you and your family to be self-sufficient for at least 3 days.

Prior to an anticipated event there is often a rush to purchase emergency supplies. Supplies may be limited, or gone at the time a disaster is upon you.

When building your kit, imagine you'll be camping in the wilderness for an extended period of time.

What would you need to be comfortable?

If you plan ahead you can have peace of mind knowing you are prepared. The following are items you should have on hand *before* a disaster occurs.

Water

You should plan on having a minimum of one gallon of water per person, per day. You should store at least a 3 day supply of water. Water for drinking should be stored in clean containers that can be tightly sealed.

If you do not have your own containers, simply purchase bottled water at your local grocery store. Your stored water supply should be kept in a cool dark place.

Do not leave water exposed to direct sunlight. Be sure to rotate your drinking water supply at least every 6 months.

Don't forget water will also be needed for pets, brushing your teeth, bathing, washing food, dishes or for general cleaning.

People who live in hot climates, children, pets, sick people and nursing mothers often require more water.

If you plan to be active or out working in the elements, you should have extra water stored. Never ration water unless told to do so.

Stocking up on water before a disaster is the best thing to do, but if you are caught off guard, there are many water sources in and around your home that can be used during an emergency.

Some of the sources below may not be safe to drink without purification. Information on purifying water can be found later in this chapter.

Utilizing these emergency resources would be a "worst case" scenario if no other water was available for an extended period of time.

Emergency Water Sources

Ice Cubes: Melt them for quick use

Bath tubs: If you anticipate a disaster, you can fill your bath tub with water. This water can be used as an extra source of drinking water, or for sanitary purposes. If stored for extended periods, be sure to purify it.

Hot water tanks: Most homes have at least a 40 gallon water tank with clean, usable water. To access the water in your hot water tank, first turn off the electric or gas supply to the water heater. Turn off the gas at the intake valve or turn off the electricity at the circuit breaker, or unplug the unit.

Open the drain at the bottom of the tank to retrieve the water. Do not turn on the gas or electricity when the tank is empty. When the water in the tank is refilled, you can then reactivate the gas or electric for heating.

Pipes: To use the water in your pipes, open (turn on) the faucet at the highest point in your house.

This lets air into the plumbing system. Now you can drain the water from the pipes through the lowest faucet in the house. If the main water valve is closed, be sure that gas used to heat the water is turned off to prevent overheating.

Water beds: These can hold up to 400 gallons, but some water beds contain toxic chemicals that are not fully removed by many purifiers. Check with the manufacturer to determine if your particular model would be safe.

If you designate a water bed in your home as an emergency resource, drain it yearly and refill it with fresh water containing two ounces of bleach per 120 gallons.

Swimming pools: Pools can provide thousands of gallons of extra usable water if needed. This is a good source of water to use for personal hygiene and cleaning but it is not safe to drink without purification. If you need to drink it, be sure to boil it first. Pools should be covered when not in use to protect the water supply.

Toilets: Your toilet tank contains usable water that can be used as a last resort. If you must use toilet water, use the water in the top tank. Do not use the bowl water. Always boil the water before use and be sure the tank does not contain any chemicals.

Remember, if water service is not available your toilet will not flush. Having extra water on hand from a source such as your bath tub will allow you to continue to use your toilet.

Simply add water to the tank to make the toilet work as normal. Another option would be the utilization of a camping toilet.

Other Water Sources: Rainwater, snow, rivers, streams, ponds, lakes, and natural springs. Avoid using water with any floating material, or an odor or dark color. Consider a rain collection barrel or similar device for extra water storage.

Never drink flood water as it may be contaminated. Natural water sources should be purified before drinking because they often contain bacteria that can make you sick.

Purifying Water

Water purification can be accomplished by boiling water in a clean container for about 5 minutes. Be sure to let it cool before drinking and keep the container covered while it is cooling.

Boiled water will taste better if you restore oxygen by pouring the water back and forth between two clean containers. This will also improve the taste of stored water.

You can also purchase water purification tablets. These are available at most stores that sell sporting goods or camping supplies.

Be sure to follow the instructions provided on the package. Water purification tablets should be included in every emergency supply kit for worst case scenarios..

Household bleach can also be used to kill microorganisms.

To purify water with bleach, use only regular household liquid bleach that contains 5.25 to 6.0 percent sodium hypochlorite (this should be noted on the label).

Do not use scented bleaches, color safe bleaches, or bleaches with added cleaners.

Use bleach from a newly opened or unopened bottle, because the potency of bleach diminishes over time.

Add 16 drops (1/8 teaspoon) of bleach per gallon of water, stir, and let stand for 30 minutes. The water should have a slight bleach odor. If it doesn't, then repeat the dosage and let stand for another 15 minutes. If it still does not smell of chlorine, discard it and find another source of water.

Emergency water supply packets are also an option. These are sealed packs of small amounts of water. They have a longer shelf life than bottled water, usually lasting up to 5 years.

Food

A 3 day supply of non-perishable food is recommended to have on hand (per person). You should select foods that do not require water, cooking or refrigeration. Items such as canned goods are excellent to keep stored (be sure to have a can opener also).

If there is no power in your home, you should consume your perishable items first.

Simple preparation is the key to successful food planning.

You should have a supply of healthy foods available that will give your energy and nutrients. You should also have comfort foods such as your favorite snacks or candy on hand.

During stressful events, the following items may help you feel better.

Other food items to consider

Protein / Fruit / Energy Bars

Dry Cereal

Vitamins

Supplements

Crackers

Be sure to include food for infants and your pets.

You can also consider purchasing military type "ready to eat" meals (also known as M.R.E'.s). These are available at military surplus stores or camping supply centers.

Consider growing a garden at your home. You can have a supply of fresh fruits and vegetables if needed.

Cooking Without a Power Source

If gas and electric service are not available in your home, you will need a heat source to prepare your food or boil water.

Consider using a barbecue grill or a camping stove. Both require fuel such as wood, charcoal or propane. Be sure to have an adequate amount of fuel prior to a disaster.

Don't wait until the last minute to stock up.

Never use these cooking appliances inside a home. Be sure you know how to properly operate them before use.

Be sure they are properly ventilated while being used.

First Aid Kit

Your basic first aid supplies should include the following:

Sterile Dressings: Use to cover wounds and stop bleeding.

Antibiotic and burn ointment: Use these to prevent infection in wounds and burns.

Adhesive bandages: Keep a variety of sizes on hand to treat a variety of wounds.

Other important medical supplies to have: Scissors, Medical Tape, Tweezers, Petroleum Jelly, Latex or other sterile gloves, eye wash solution.

Prescription medications and supplies: Do not wait until you run out of your prescriptions. Keep an adequate supply of medication in case you do not have access to a pharmacy if evacuated. Stores may be destroyed or inaccessible.

Non-Prescription Medication: Keep a supply of pain relievers, anti-diarrhea medication, laxatives and antacids.

Radio: A portable radio is good to have so you can monitor news broadcasts or emergency alerts. Be sure to have batteries on hand. You can also purchase radios that are wind up or solar powered so you do not need batteries.

NOAA Weather Radio: Consider purchasing one of these radios. You can program the radio to receive emergency warnings for your specific area from the National Weather Service. These are "all hazards" radios that will provide you with the most comprehensive information during an event. They are available for purchase at most department stores.

Flashlights: Everyone in your home should have one. Keep a supply of fresh batteries for the lights. Be sure the batteries are the correct size and type for your lights. You can also consider purchasing wind up flashlights that do not require batteries.

Candles: These can be an efficient source of lighting, but be sure to have matches or a lighter also. Do not leave candles unattended while burning.

Glow Sticks: Also known as "chem-lights", these are very useful to have in your kit. Glow sticks provide a non-flammable, heatless light source. Good quality sticks give off 8 – 12 hours of bright light. White sticks can be used for emergency lighting.

Other colors could be used to signal help if needed. These are inexpensive and have an excellent shelf life.

Blankets: If heating is not available you should have extra blankets or a sleeping bag to keep warm. Emergency blankets are another option. Made of Mylar, emergency blankets come in compact pocket sized carry cases.

When opened, they are large enough to wrap a person. These blankets can retain up to 90% of a person's body heat. They can also serve as a temporary shelter when outside. Because of their bright sliver color, they can also be used for emergency signaling.

Extra Clothing: Be prepared for varying weather conditions and damaged or wet clothes. Have at least one change of clothing for each person in your emergency kit appropriate for your climate.

Tools: Duct tape, a tarp, hammer, screw driver, wrench, pliers, and fire extinguisher. Every emergency kit should have tools in case some minor repairs are required.

Additional Items

Toilet paper

Infant diapers / wet wipes

Feminine supplies

Deodorant

Toothbrush / toothpaste

Garbage bags

Insect repellent

Money

Consider having some cash on hand. If there is no power, ATM's and store credit card readers will not work. Electronic transactions may not be an option. If you are lucky enough to have access to shopping in a disaster, merchants will most likely only accept cash.

Entertainment

It is also important to have something to keep you and your family occupied. Have some books, toys or games available, especially for children. If your children enjoy electronic games, be sure to have batteries for those too.

The items for your emergency kit should be kept together in a carrying case that is easily accessible. You can also make a smaller kit to be carried in a car. Be sure to update the items in your kit as the needs of your family change.

Also be sure to check the expiration dates of items in your kits to maintain a fresh supply. Be sure everyone in your family knows where your emergency kit is located.

Each member of your family may want to build their own kits. If you permit this, just ensure everyone has the needed essentials.

Backup Power Options

Consider the purchase of a power generator. Generators are usually gas powered and can provide many hours of electricity. Some are small and portable, intended for light use. Others are large and can fully power homes or businesses.

If you have critical power requirements such as the use of life sustaining medical devices or computer systems, a generator can be invaluable. Contact your local hardware store for more information about generators.

Solar power is another option for disaster planning. Solar panels use the power of sunlight to create energy. Solar panels come in a variety of sizes depending on your energy needs.

Solar can be an expensive option, but having self-generating power can save you money over time. Solar power also helps the environment as it does not create any harmful emissions.

CHAPTER 3

When Disaster Strikes

If there is an impending event you will be notified by authorities. The most common alert notification is the Emergency Alert System. This is the warning tones heard on TV and radio stations which are followed by instructions. You may also be alerted by warning sirens, weather radios, or by telephone.

If time permits, newspapers or magazines may also provide warning information. These warnings will inform you as to whether you should stay where you are, or go somewhere else for safety. You should be sure to follow the instructions provided by authorities to ensure your safety.

When a disaster occurs, the first responders to the scene will be your local police, fire and emergency medical providers. If you live in a large city, you will have many resources at your disposal. However, if you live in a rural area or small town, services are often limited.

Responders will have many duties to attend to. There may be fires, safety hazards or many rescues to attend to. If the event is a terrorist incident or suspicious in nature, the area will also be a crime scene.

During a small scale event, resources will easily be overwhelmed. Even large cities can become overwhelmed with an incident.

One of the most important factors to consider when developing your emergency plan is the fact that you may be on your own for a short time when a disaster occurs. You may not have the luxury of calling 9-1-1 for assistance.

Government agencies understand this. Even the government needs to have a plan in place to assist them when needed, because there simply aren't enough responders to help everyone during a major incident.

Cities both large and small must rely on what is called a mutual aid agreement. This is a plan that is arranged long before a disaster strikes.

It allows public safety agencies to rely on other surrounding agencies to provide extra assistance when needed.

Hospitals must also have a similar plan in place. Imagine a rural hospital with only a few beds having to handle a mass casualty event. Small facilities simply could not handle the overload of patients.

Cities and organizations, like individuals, need to always have a backup plan.

When local resources are overwhelmed, the next level of assistance will come from the state. State resources may include state law enforcement or fire agencies.

These resources may be delayed do the unforeseen conditions in an emergency, or they may be coming from a far distance. If an emergency is serious enough, the Governor of the state can also activate National Guard units to respond for assistance.

If state agencies become overwhelmed the Governor can also request help from other states. If the disaster extends beyond the response of available state resources, the Governor can declare a state of emergency which will then start the process of assistance from the federal government.

Federal Response

Federal resources cannot get involved until after local and state resources have been overwhelmed and the Governor has declared a state of emergency.

After a state Governor has declared a state of emergency, the President can then authorize federal response assistance and resources to be directed to the disaster area.

Federal assistance includes the resources of the Federal Emergency Management Agency. Assistance may come in the form of additional emergency responders, supplies or financial aid for agencies involved in the response.

Federal resources may also provide financial assistance to help with the recovery effort after the event is over. Federal resources may take up to 3 days to arrive at the disaster site.

This is why you need to be prepared to take care of yourself. Having adequate emergency supplies will allow you to sustain yourself during this period if help is not immediately available.

Evacuation

Before, or during a disaster, you may need to be evacuated for your safety. Evacuations are more common than most people think. Evacuations occur hundreds of times each year due to storms, fires, industrial accidents or hazardous chemical spills.

You may have advance warning to evacuate in some situations. Some events such as hurricanes can allow you advance notice of a day or two. Other fast acting situations will not give any warning. You may need to leave with only a moment notice.

This is why you should prepare ahead of time and have your emergency kit ready to go.

You may be required to go to a shelter for your protection. Shelters are often located in places such as school gymnasiums, churches or other buildings able to accommodate large groups of people with protection from the threat. You will alerted by authorities as to what you should do.

The decision to evacuate will be based on the perceived threat. Your individual situation may vary depending on your location, your shelter and the intensity of the pending incident. Be sure to follow all instructions provided to minimize risk of injury or property damage.

If you are evacuating on your own, be sure to follow instructions for the recommended safest route out of the affected area. Do not take short cuts as the route may be inaccessible or potentially dangerous.

Before you leave your home, be sure it is secured. Close the windows and lock your doors. If you have time and if you are advised to do so, shut off your water, gas and electricity.

Learn how to shut off your utilities before a disaster occurs. Be sure to bring your emergency supply kit and other important items.

If possible, let others know where you are going and which route you are taking. It is common for people to want to head into the disaster area to get to loved ones or to provide help. This may be dangerous and could potentially cause more problems. Avoid the disaster area if possible.

Sheltering In Place

Some types of chemical or industrial accidents or terrorist attacks may make it unsafe to leave your home or business. Evacuating could take too long or it could put you in harm's way. You may be required to shelter in place.

Shelter in place means to stay where you are during an emergency. This may be a better alternative than removing you from a disaster area.

Usually if you are told to shelter in place it will only be for a few hours, though it could be longer. This is why you need to be prepared. Ask yourself if you'd be able to sustain yourself.

If you could not leave your home or business right now, would you be able to shelter in place for an extended period of time? Would you be prepared?

Create a Safe Room

Designate a room in your home to serve as your safe room. The best room to use is one with the fewest windows and doors. You should keep your emergency supply kit in your safe room. If told to shelter in place, go to your safe room immediately.

Monitor a radio or television for information. Do not leave your home until you are told it is safe to do so.

Different incidents require different sheltering methods. Refer to chapter 7 for more information.

Chapter 4

After The Disaster

After a disaster there will be chaos, confusion and fear. Roads may be closed or inaccessible as a result of damage or debris.

Transportation facilities and hospitals may be shut down, damaged or destroyed. Communications will most likely be affected. During the event, you may be stranded where you are.

A perfect example of this was during Hurricane Katrina in 2005. Residents and visitors who did not evacuate were stranded when roads in and out of the city were cut off.

During the terrorist attacks of September 11th 2001, every airport in the United States was closed. Every airplane in the sky was forced to land where ever they were. Many travelers were stranded in cities far from home for an extended period of time.

With so many people stranded, telephone lines were overwhelmed by hundreds of thousands of callers trying to communicate with friends and family.

With roads and highways closed or inaccessible, you may not be able to make it back to your home or you may not be able to leave home if you are sheltered in place. At the same time, rescuers may not be able to get to you in a timely manner.

This is why it is very important to have an emergency kit in your home, as well as in your vehicle. You need to be able to take care of yourself in an emergency.

The most important concern after a disaster should be the health and safety of you and your family. Remain calm and assess the situation. A clear mind will allow for better decision making.

Emergency responders will make every effort possible to save lives, but as mentioned previously, there may not be enough responders to help all the injured. You may be the one who provides assistance and care to others.

Aiding the Injured

Checking for injuries and accounting for friends and loved ones should be your first priority. Ensure that you are in a safe position before attempting first aid so you will not cause further injury.

Be aware of hazards such as debris, wires, fire or structural damage. Always check your surroundings. You can't help others if you become injured further.

If you have access to 9-1-1 or medical facilities, seek professional help immediately for injuries. If you do not have immediate access to assistance, you should do your best to prevent further injury.

Follow up with professional care as soon as possible to prevent infection or other complications.

You should only attempt to provide first aid for the skills and knowledge you have been trained on.

This book is not meant to serve as a first aid training guide. You should attend an in-person training course to improve your first aid knowledge and skills.

Triage

When rescuers arrive at the scene of a disaster or mass casualty incident, they must do what is known as triage. Triage is the quick assessment of injuries to determine who is in the most immediate need of help.

Triage is also routinely used in hospitals and walk in care clinics to determine who needs assistance first.

When a rescuer checks patients in a mass casualty incident, they are assigned a color coded tag.

In civilian response, the four colors typically used are green, yellow, red and black.

Each color represents the level of emergency care needed. Patients with the most serious injuries will be treated first.

Those with minor injuries can wait to seek medical attention.

Triage Color Codes

Black: Used for those who are deceased, or who will most likely not survive, even with rapid emergency care.

Red: Used for those with serious life threatening injuries. These patients may not survive without immediate emergency care.

Yellow: Used for patients with more serious, but non-life threatening injuries. These patients can wait for treatment.

Green: Used for patients with minor injuries. These patients do not require immediate emergency care or treatment.

Medical facilities and rescuers will be overwhelmed in a major mass casualty incident. If you are not seriously injured, let rescuers tend to those who are.

With basic first aid skills, you may be able to help yourself or others. This will allow rescuers to handle an incident more efficiently.

Basic First Aid

Note: In order to avoid possible health contamination risks, always use latex or rubber gloves. It is always best to attend a first aid course so you can learn the proper techniques to help yourself and others in emergency situations.

First: Check for any obvious injuries.

Unconscious / Not Breathing

Do not attempt to move a trapped, seriously injured or unconscious person unless they are in immediate danger of death or further serious injury.

If you must move an injured or unconscious person, first stabilize the neck and back, then call for help immediately if you can.

Shake the person and ask "are you okay" to see if you can get a response. If there is no response, remain calm and do a patient assessment.

If you find an unconscious person, remember your "ABC"s (Airway / Breathing / Circulation):

A: Be sure to check the **airway** for any obstructions. If there are any foreign objects, clear them with a finger sweep.

B: Place one hand on the victim's forehead. Carefully raise the chin back. Is the person **breathing**? Place your ear next to the victim's mouth and listen for breath sounds. Look for any rise or movement in the chest.

C: Does the person have **circulation** (a pulse)?

If the person is not breathing or does not have a pulse, carefully position the victim to administer CPR (Cardiopulmonary Resuscitation).

Procedures for CPR change periodically. You should attend a CPR training course to ensure your knowledge of the most current CPR techniques. If you have access to an Automatic External Defibrillator (AED), this is a great life-saving tool.

An AED is a device used to restart the heart. Many CPR courses will also instruct you on the use of these devices.

Bleeding: Attempt to control bleeding through the use of direct pressure. Apply constant pressure on the wound using a towel or dressing. Use sterile dressings if possible.

Untreated bleeding can lead to shock. Proper wound management and cleaning is best done by professional medical staff. If the bleeding gets worse or cannot be controlled, seek professional help as soon as possible.

Broken Bones: Do not try to straighten an extremity if it is deformed or if bones are protruding. If there is any bleeding, try to control it. Keep the injury in the position where it is and try to stabilize it.

If medical assistance is not readily available, use padding or a splint to keep it from moving. If you are able to elevate the injured extremity without causing further injury, do so to prevent swelling.

Put ice on the injury, but not directly on the skin (place the ice in a plastic bag or towel). Keep the ice on the injury for 20 minutes, then take it off for 20 minutes, then repeat.

Over the counter pain killers can help to ease the pain.

If the person feels faint or if breathing is short or rapid, lay the person down with the head slightly lower than the trunk and, if possible, elevate the legs.

Burns: Minor burns (slightly reddened skin with no blisters) can be treated with a topical burn ointment or spray. Use water to cool the burn. Over the counter pain killers can be used to ease the pain of minor burns.

If there is charring, blistering or if skin is peeling, these are indicators of a serious injury and complications are likely. Seek professional medical attention as soon as possible.

Any burns to the face, hands, feet or genital area should also be treated by a professional.

Do not apply butter or oils to burns. Cover the wound with sterile dressings. Wear loose fitting clothing while burns are healing.

Shock: Shock can be a serious, life threatening medical condition. Shock is caused by decreased blood flow to the brain and other extremities.

Look for signs of altered mental state, empty stare in the eyes, rapid shallow breathing and cool, clammy skin.

Ensure the injured person has a clear airway. Reassure the person and have them lie down with the feet elevated. Prevent the loss the body heat with a blanket.

Be sure the victim does not become overheated.

Do not attempt to give an unconscious person anything by mouth.

If there is bleeding, it needs to be controlled. If there is vomiting, roll the victim to one side and sweep the vomit from his or her mouth with your fingers.

Continue to check on the victim until medical assistance can be obtained.

Checking Your Home

If it is safe to go outside, walk around the exterior of your home to check for structural damage. This should also be done if returning home from an evacuation center.

If your home has suffered any flood, fire or storm damage, stay out. If you have any doubts about the stability of your structure, do not re-enter it until it has been inspected by a professional.

If authorities have declared a home or building to be unsafe, stay out of it. Debris or potentially contaminated materials may also be present.

Safety Issues

Be aware of new safety issues created by the disaster. Watch for washed out roads, damaged buildings, contaminated water, broken glass, damaged electrical wiring, and slippery floors.

Always wear protective clothing, sturdy work boots and gloves. If handling debris, wear safety glasses also.

If communications permit, advise your local authorities about any health and safety issues. Chemical spills, downed power lines, washed out roads, and dead animals are concerns that should be promptly addressed.

Use the phone only to report hazards or life-threatening emergencies. Stay off the streets. If you must go out, watch for fallen objects; downed electrical wires, damaged walls, bridges, roads, and sidewalks.

Gas Leaks

If your home or business utilizes natural gas service, leaks are a major hazard.

If you hear a hissing or roaring sound around gas meters or appliances, you may have a leak.

Other signs of a leak include appliances failing to ignite, bubbling puddles of water in your yard or around gas meters and dead vegetation around your gas meter.

If you detect the pungent odor of rotten eggs, this is an additive in natural gas to let you know of a leak. If you notice any of these indicators, leave the area immediately and notify 911 or your local gas service authority.

Do not turn on light switches or use your phone in the area of a possible leak and do not use lighters, matches or any other open flame.

Do not reenter the structure until you are told it is safe to do so.

Other Home Hazards

Watch out for animals, especially poisonous snakes. Wear long pants, boots and gloves. Use a stick to poke through debris. Be aware of an increase in insects as well. Remove standing water in yards as this is a breeding ground for mosquitoes.

What Else?

What if you cannot find your family?

FEMA established the National Emergency Family Registry and Locator System (NEFRLS). This was developed to help reunite families separated during a disaster.

The NEFRLS system enables displaced individuals the ability to enter personal information into a website database so that they can be located by others during a disaster.

Individuals and families can register online at www.fema.gov. If children 21 years old or younger become separated, FEMA will activate the National Emergency Child Locator Center to help families, local and tribal governments, and law enforcement agencies track and locate children separated from their parents or guardians because of the disaster.

This service is managed by the National Center for Missing and Exploited Children, with support from FEMA. Call centers may be reached at 1-800-588-9822, 24 hours a day when it is activated.

The American Red Cross also maintains a database to help relocate family members.

As mentioned in the planning section, arrange for third party contacts away from the disaster area. Check in with this person so everyone will be accounted for.

The Red Cross and other organizations will be at the disaster site. Advise authorities of missing persons so rescuers can be made aware.

Insurance

Also be sure to contact your insurance agent after a disaster. They will assess the damage and assist you with getting back to a normal life.

Agencies at the disaster location can provide guidance regarding temporary housing and financial assistance.

Be sure your policies provide adequate coverage and be sure they are paid and up to date *before* a disaster strikes.

Health

Be aware of exhaustion. Don't try to do too much at once.

Set priorities and pace yourself.

Get enough rest, eat well and drink plenty of clean water.

Wash your hands thoroughly with soap and water often when working in or around debris.

Wear study boots or shoes to protect your feet from hazards.

Pay attention to the environmental conditions and dress accordingly.

CHAPTER 5

Disaster Related Stress

Recovering from a disaster is usually a gradual process. Physical safety is always a primary issue, but mental health often gets overlooked.

This section offers some general advice on steps you can take after disaster strikes in order to begin getting your home, your community, and your life back to normal.

Everyone who sees or experiences a disaster will be affected by it in some way. It is perfectly normal to feel concerned or anxious about your own safety and the safety of your family and friends.

Sadness, confusion, grief, anger and frustration are normal emotional reactions to an abnormal event.

Stress is a common problem following disaster. How you deal with your stress will determine how you get through the recovery process. It is often easy to overlook emotional stress, as everyone experiences disaster differently.

Anyone, regardless of age or background can be affected by stress. Some people will openly express feelings, but others may contain them. It is extremely important that you recognize the symptoms of someone in emotional distress.

By recognizing the symptoms, you may be able to help get a life back to normal. Persons showing signs of stress should seek assistance as soon as possible to minimize the effects.

The sooner you seek treatment, the sooner you'll get things back to normal.

Symptoms of Stress

Difficulty with communicating

Excessive anxiety

Having trouble sleeping or having nightmares

Easily angered or frustrated

Increased use of drugs or alcohol

Limited attention span

Poor or declining work performance

Persistent headaches or stomach problems

Tunnel vision or muffled hearing

Little or no energy

Disorientation or confusion

Difficulty concentrating on simple tasks

Loss of appetite or overeating

General depression or sadness

Feelings of hopelessness

Severe mood swings.

Guilt or self-doubt that overwhelms you

If you or someone you know has these symptoms, there are things you can do. Talk with someone and tell them about your feelings.

Discussing your feelings can help you recover faster. Although it may be difficult, it is important to do so.

Do not be embarrassed about seeking help from a professional counselor who deals with disaster related stress. Stress is normal.

Getting help when you need it is not a weakness. You can get counseling help from community groups, local faith-based organizations, volunteer agencies, or professional counselors.

You can also speak with your family physician, as there may also be other underlying medical issues related to the stress. Post-traumatic stress disorder (PTSD) is quite common, as well as depression. The good thing is that these are treatable.

FEMA, state and local governments may also provide crisis counseling assistance in areas affected by disaster. Rescue workers should especially watch for signs of stress in themselves and co-workers during and after an incident.

You do not have to be directly involved with a disaster to experience disaster stress. Symptoms of second hand exposure can come from media coverage or worry.

People who experience a disaster indirectly can show the same symptoms as those who are directly affected. Even just planning for disaster can be stressful. Worry can easily overwhelm you if you let it.

Dealing with your emotional stress is just as important as making an emergency kit. You can improve your own physical and emotional well-being by eating healthy foods, getting adequate rest and exercising on a regular basis.

Take time to relax. Try to get back to a normal routine after a disaster. Spend quality time with family and friends and limit demanding activities. Try to do things that make you happy.

Children and Disasters

Children are of special concern in the aftermath of disasters. Disasters can be traumatic events for children, even if they were not directly affected by it.

Children may be more prone to fear and anxiety than adults because they do not understand why disasters occur. Educate children about the different types of disasters.

If a child has questions about a disaster, answer them truthfully. Remind them it is okay to be scared. Be sure to comfort them to ease the anxiety. It is important for adults to discuss feelings about disaster with children.

Children's anxiety levels can increase by simply hearing parents or teachers talk about events. Seeing images of disaster on television can add to the anxiety.

It is very important for parents and teachers to recognize and understand the symptoms of emotional stress.

Kids are very observant. They will notice fear, anxiety and sadness in adults. Parents can help make disasters less stressful for children by discussing their own thoughts, feelings and fears. If parents share feelings, they can help children while managing their own feelings and fears.

Some children may not want to talk about their feelings. Offer other ways of expressing feelings such as drawing a picture or telling a story. Remain positive and validate the feelings expressed. A major fear of those involved in an incident is that it will happen again.

Children can experience many of the same stress symptoms as adults. In addition to fear and sadness, children may also demonstrate behavioral problems. Young children may experience bed wetting, sleep problems, and separation anxiety.

Older children may show anger, aggression and withdrawal. Both younger and older children may have difficulty with performance in school. Emotional reactions to disasters are often brief for most children, but some may be at risk for longer lasting psychological issues based on other major risk factors or history.

Direct Exposure or Involvement

Fear and anxiety are to be expected in children. Those who directly experience events such as sustaining personal injury, witnessing injuries or death or being involved in a life threatening experience will have a higher risk of emotional distress and long term issues.

It is critical that these children be monitored for problems. If a child experiences the loss of a friend or family member due to a disaster, it can be even more of a traumatic emotional event.

On-Going Stress

Being evacuated from home, losing personal property and having to stay in temporary housing can be a major shock to a child. Children may not understand why things are changing.

They will be in unfamiliar situations with people they may not know. This is very uncomfortable for adults, but more so for kids. Observed parental stress will add to the emotional problems of children.

Post disaster anxiety and stress in children can increase through reminders of the event. For those directly involved in a disaster, certain triggers can bring back memories of the event.

Photos, media coverage, sirens, storms or other related reminders can bring back upsetting feelings. Children with prior history of traumatic events or severe stress may have an increase in these feelings. Try to be aware of these triggers and limit them as best you can until the child can better handle their emotions.

Depending on the risk factors above, most distressing responses in children are often temporary. In the absence of a life threatening event, personal injury, or the loss of loved ones, most emotional symptoms will go away with time. Seek professional help if they do not seem to be going away.

Parents are the first line of support for children coping with disaster. Engage your family and involve children in drills and the emergency planning process. Let them know you have a plan to keep them safe. Reassure them that schools and other adults are also developing plans to keep everyone safe.

Let them know you are doing everything you can to take care of them and that everything will be okay. Just as with adults, children need to learn to prepare for disasters. Reassure them you are doing what is needed by planning and creating an emergency kit. Allow them to participate in the process.

Remain calm and stay positive. Try to show that you are in control and prepared. Your confidence and emotional well-being will extend to your children.

Take your children to visit a police or fire station. Let them meet rescuers and allow them to learn about rescue equipment. All children are curious about these things.

Sometimes children are afraid of police or firefighters because they have never encountered them up close. Building trust can be a major step in overcoming anxiety about emergencies. In addition, it may help to reassure them someone is there watching out when disasters happen.

CHAPTER 6

Severe Weather / Natural Threats

Weather threats are a danger every one of us will face at some time in our lives. The good thing about weather events is that you will usually have warning before they strike.

Warnings will give you time to prepare. If you fail to act upon the warnings, you may face danger. Many people are unaware of the dangers that hazardous weather presents.

Those who do not listen to warnings are the ones who usually suffer the most. With proper precautions, it is possible to make it through a hazardous natural event without incident.

Know your warnings and be sure to follow them.

Watch: Watches are issued when weather conditions exist that could create a hazard. You should be aware of the potential hazard and begin to take precautions.

Warning: A warning is issued when a specific weather threat is occurring. If a warning is issued, you may be in immediate danger. You should follow the instructions given to protect yourself.

The following pages will guide you through the dangers of specific natural hazards.

Avalanche

Avalanches are large amounts of rapidly moving snow that occur in mountainous terrain. Avalanches are made of snow which differentiates them from landslides.

Avalanches are always caused by external stress on the snow pack. They claim more than 150 lives worldwide every year. Thousands of other people have been injured or partially buried.

To prevent avalanches, do not ski, hike or snowmobile in avalanche prone areas. Assess hazardous areas and consult with area mapping agencies to determine your risk before entering dangerous areas.

If you are caught in an avalanche, try to take cover behind large trees or rocks. Crouch low, cover your mouth and nose and turn away from the avalanche. If you are caught in the snow pack, thrust and kick upward to get to the surface of the snow.

Many avalanche deaths are caused by suffocation. As the snow pack slows, pull your arms and hands toward your face to create an air space.

When the slide stops, try to remain calm. Yell for help if rescuers are near, but conserve your energy. Try to thrust an arm to the surface and try to dig yourself out.

For more information, consult local guides for maximum safety. If you are planning a backcountry adventure, carry a portable shovel and adequate supplies with you. You can also carry a collapsible ski pole probe.

These are poles that can be pieced together to aid in finding a buried victim. Avalanche beacons can also be carried. These are transmitters that emit a signal to help rescuers locate trapped victims.

If travelling through avalanche prone areas, always let someone know where you're going and when you'll be back.

Avoid back country travel when you are alone.

Blackouts / Power Outages

Blackouts, or power outages can be caused by a variety of factors. They can be caused by faults, or problems at power stations.

They may also be caused by damage to power transmission lines (poles and wires being knocked down or struck by lightning), overloaded power grids, or short circuits.

Most power outages are only temporary, lasting just a few minutes or hours. In a large disaster, the outages may last longer.

To prepare for outages, have a working flashlight with good batteries accessible. Candles are also a good idea. Remember to have matches or a lighter available.

Glow sticks are a great option. They can provide many hours of safe bright light and do not require fuel or batteries.

Blackouts pose a concern for electronic items. To protect valuable computers and other electronics, invest in a quality surge protector.

Keep your refrigerator and freezer doors closed as long as possible to keep your food cold.

Refer to page 40 for tips on preparing food without power. Also refer to page 43 for backup power options.

During the winter, be prepared to keep warn without

Earthquakes

Earthquakes are caused by the movement of plates deep within the Earth's surface. These plates move constantly and rub against each other. The plates occasionally shift with great force, causing a quake. A fault line is the area where the rocks are sliding past each other.

The movement in the fault lines often can cause cracks in the Earth's surface. Some fault lines are more active than others, such as the San Andreas Fault in southern California. Earthquakes can often trigger Tsunami's.

There are more than a million recorded earthquakes each year. Earthquakes can occur anywhere. Most people think of California when you mention earthquakes.

However, in 1811 and 1812, three quakes believed to be some of the largest and most violent in US history were actually centered in an area of southeast Missouri known as New Madrid.

The earthquake forcibly shook the ground in a 50,000 square mile area. With minimal communication and a sparse population, there was no way of knowing how many people were injured or killed, or how many structures were destroyed.

Seismograph equipment was not yet in use, so there was no way of knowing the true intensity. There were reports of church bells ringing in Philadelphia because of the shaking. Shaking was also said to have been felt in Boston, New York and Norfolk, Virginia.

The New Madrid Fault is still active today. It is believed the area of southeast Missouri will be the center of a major earthquake sometime in the near future. If a major quake should occur, the urban areas of Memphis Tennessee, Little Rock Arkansas and St. Louis Missouri could be severely affected.

Earthquakes can strike anywhere. You should be aware of the hazards, no matter where you live.

What to do if an earthquake strikes

If you are inside during an earthquake, remain calm, drop to the ground and seek cover under something such as a sturdy desk or table. Try to hang on to something. Protect your head with a pillow or your hands.

Stay where you are and do not try to move around until the shaking is over. If you are outside seek an open area. Try to stay away from buildings, trees and power lines.

Check for injuries then inspect your home after the shaking has stopped. Be aware of aftershocks that may occur. If your home is damaged, stay out of it until it has been inspected by a professional.

Beware of downed power lines, damaged utilities and other structural damage or debris.

Falling objects are a threat during earthquakes. Bolt book shelves or other tall furniture to a wall. Place heavy or large items on lower shelves. Secure cupboards and cabinets with latches that prevent them from opening during a quake.

Do not hang pictures or other items over your bed.

Brace hanging light fixtures.

Secure your water heater by strapping it to wall studs.

Floods

Floods are the most common natural disaster in the United States. Flooding can occur when there are heavy rains or excessive melting snow. Floods can also occur from high ocean tides, improper urban storm drainage, damaged levees or broken dams.

Rivers, streams and lakes may overflow due to the excessive water amounts. At risk locations include coastal regions, areas adjacent to rivers, streams, or lakes, dry river beds and low lying areas such as valleys.

On average, floods kill over 140 people each year and cause over $6 billion dollars in property damage. Flooding can occur in any part of our nation at any time of the year.

If flooding is anticipated, go to higher ground. Flash flooding is also a serious risk. If heavy rains are expected, avoid dry river beds, creeks, streams and valleys during a storm.

Flood water can move rapidly and without warning. It may not be raining where you are, but water can flow from far away, especially in mountainous areas. Dry areas can turn into raging rivers in only a matter of minutes.

Do NOT attempt to drive through flooded areas. Only 6 inches of moving water can knock you off your feet. 2 feet of moving water will cause your car to float. Water levels are often difficult to judge.

Don't take the chance of driving through deep water. If a road appears to be flooded, take another route. Pay attention to closed road signs.

If your home is prone to flooding, raise up items such as furnaces, electrical boxes and water heaters. Move furniture, electronics and valuables to a higher area of your home.

Excessive Heat

Heat exhaustion and heat stroke are serious conditions caused by exposure to excessive heat. The human body can normally regulate its temperature in hot weather by sweating. In excessive heat your body can't keep up and becomes overloaded.

Infants, young children, the elderly and overweight people are the most vulnerable to heat related problems. Heat related illnesses are common, but they can be prevented.

The easiest way to prevent heat problems is to stay hydrated by drinking water and avoid excessive time in the heat. It does not take long to become dehydrated. It is very important to drink water before, during after being exposed to hot weather.

Do your best to stay cool.

Two main effects of excessive heat exposure are Heat Stroke and Heat Exhaustion. Both can be life threatening if not treated.

Warning Signs of Heat Stroke

An extremely high body temperature (above 103°F)

Red, hot, and dry skin (no sweating)

Rapid, strong pulse

Throbbing headache

Dizziness / Nausea

Confusion

Unconsciousness

Heat stroke is a very serious condition. These symptoms may be signs of a life threatening emergency. If you witness someone with these symptoms, seek professional medical assistance immediately.

Move the victim to a shady area. Cool the victim rapidly, using whatever methods you can. For example, immerse the victim in a tub of cool water; place the person in a cool shower; spray the victim with cool water from a garden hose; sponge the person with cool water; or if the humidity is low, wrap the victim in a cool, wet sheet and fan the patient vigorously.

Monitor body temperature and continue cooling efforts until the body temperature drops to 101-102°F.

If emergency medical personnel are delayed, call a hospital emergency room for further instructions. If communications are not available, do your best to keep the patient cool until help arrives.

Do not give the victim any beverages that contain alcohol. Allow them to drink cool water if they are alert and conscious. Do not attempt to give liquids to an unconscious person.

Heat Exhaustion

Heat exhaustion can develop after several days of exposure to high temperatures and inadequate or unbalanced replacement of fluids. Those most prone to heat exhaustion are elderly people, those with high blood pressure, and those working or exercising in a hot environment.

Hundreds of people die from heat exhaustion each year because they failed to take proper care of themselves.

Heat exhaustion is preventable. If you need to work or exercise outside, do so during the early morning or late night when temperatures are coolest.

Be sure to take breaks to cool down and drink lots of water. Check on the elderly when extreme temperatures are present.

Beware of warnings signs to prevent heat related health problems before they get worse.

Warning signs of heat exhaustion

Heavy sweating

Paleness

Muscle cramps

Tiredness

Weakness

Dizziness

Headache

Nausea or vomiting

Fainting

The skin may be cool and moist. The pulse rate will be fast and weak, and breathing will be fast and shallow.

If heat exhaustion is untreated, it may progress to heat stroke.

Seek medical attention if symptoms worsen or if they last longer than one hour.

It is important to try to cool the body.

Drink cool, nonalcoholic beverages and seek an air-conditioned environment.

Wear lightweight clothing.

Get adequate rest.

Take a cool shower, bath, or sponge bath.

Have your air conditioning system inspected regularly to ensure it running at peak efficiency.

Also consider the use of fans to improve comfort and reduce cooling costs.

Hurricanes

Hurricanes are huge storms that form over warm ocean waters. These storms can be up to 600 miles across and can have winds averaging 75 – 200 miles per hour.

Storms gain strength over the open ocean. As they approach land, they dump huge amounts of rain and can cause substantial wind damage. The storms often affect large areas across many states.

Flooding is a result of high tides and excessive rain. The storms lose power as they move ashore but often leave a trail of destruction.

Strength of hurricanes can vary from a category 1 to category 5.

The following criteria describes hurricane ratings:

Category 1: wind speeds 74-95 mph
Category 2: wind speeds 96-110 mph
Category 3: wind speeds 111-130 mph
Category 4: wind speeds 131-155 mph
Category 5: wind speeds over 155 mph

Anything below a category 1 considered a tropical storm.

Even though it's not considered a hurricane, tropical storms can still cause damage, injury and flooding.

A hurricane watch is issued when conditions exist with sustained winds of 74 mph or greater in your area within the next 36 hours.

 A hurricane warning is issued when hurricane conditions are expected in your area within 24 hours.

Flood warnings or watches may be issued as well as small craft advisories. If you are on a boat you should get to land or remain on shore during a warning period.

Depending on the size of the storm, rain can be very heavy and persistent for many days. When a hurricane reaches land, it often reduces in size and strength, but flooding will still be an ongoing issue.

If you anticipate a hurricane, secure any items on your property that could blow away or cause damage. Board up or protect windows. If flooding is expected, go further inland or go to higher ground.

You may be required to evacuate from locations in the path of the storm or in flood prone areas. Monitor warnings for instructions. Follow directions if you are told to evacuate.

Do not drive through flooded areas and be aware of debris in the roadway. Maintain extra vigilance for looters in storm damaged or vacated areas.

Landslides

Landslides can be caused by a variety of unstable material (mud, rocks or other debris) on a sloped surface. Mudslides caused by heavy rains or snow often cause problems.

Gravity may cause loose rocks to fall, causing a slide. Groundwater, erosion or loss of vegetation on slopes can also cause a normally stable area to become unstable.

Homes that are built on or near slopes and cliffs are more prone to slides. If you live in a landslide prone area, contact a professional (civil engineer) for advice on landslide management. There may corrective measures you can make to prevent problems.

If your home is in the path of an impending landslide, evacuate immediately. If you cannot evacuate, get on the floor, curl into a tight ball and protect your head.

Try to get out of the path of a landslide. After a slide, check your home for structural damage. Also check the area around your home for erosion damage and broken utility lines.

Monitor warnings for instructions during a storm or during a landslide event.

Use caution when traveling through areas where landslides may occur. If a road is closed, find another route.

Thunderstorms

About 2,000 thunderstorms occur every day somewhere on the Earth, causing about 100 strikes of cloud to ground lightning every second. They can occur during any season and in any location.

Thunderstorms are formed by rapidly rising unstable warm moist air. These storms can cause strong wind gusts, heavy rains and hail. The biggest danger in a thunderstorm comes from lightning.

Lightning is a large discharge of electricity. Within a thundercloud, small bits of ice bump into each other as they move around in the atmosphere. Lightning is believed to be caused by the collisions of these ice crystals. As they collide, they create an electric charge. After a while, the whole cloud fills up with electrical charges.

The positive charges (protons) form at the top of the cloud and the negative charges (electrons) form at the bottom of the cloud. Because opposites attract, this causes a positive charge to build up on the ground beneath the cloud. The electrical charge on the ground concentrates around anything that rises up, such as mountains, people, or trees.

The charge coming up from these points eventually connects with a charge reaching down from the clouds thus creating a lightning bolt. A lightning bolt can travel at speeds up to 22,000 miles per hour (36,000 km/h) and has a temperature of about 50,000 degrees (F).

Thunder is caused by lightning. When a lightning bolt travels from the cloud to the ground it actually opens up a small hole in the air, called a channel.

Once the light has gone through, the air collapses back in and creates a sound wave that we hear as thunder. The reason we see lightning before we hear thunder is because light travels faster than sound.

Thunder can typically be heard within about 15 miles of its source. Lightning can be seen from as far away as 100 miles.

If you can hear thunder, you may be in danger of getting struck by lightning. If you are outside during a storm, seek shelter immediately. If you are outside during a storm and you can feel your hair stand on end or your skin starts to tingle, lightning may be about to strike.

Get down on your hands and knees and keep your head tucked in. Do not lie flat, because it can give the lightning a better chance of striking you.

On average, lightning kills more people each year than hurricanes and tornadoes. You can estimate how far away a storm is by counting the number of seconds between when you see the lightning and hear the thunder.

Take the number of seconds then divide by 5. This will tell you the storm distance in miles. For example: If you counted 10 seconds between the lightning and the thunder, the lightning would be 2 miles away.

During a Thunderstorm

Seek cover inside a building, home or other suitable shelter until the storm has passed.

Shut off electrical devices to prevent damage from power surges. Protect electronics with a surge protection device.

Do not swim during a storm. If you are in water, get out immediately. Do not take a shower or a bath during a storm. Electricity can be carried through water and metal pipes.

Do not use wired telephones because lightning can be carried through the wires.

Tornadoes

A tornado is a violently rotating column of air extending from a thunderstorm to the ground. Most tornadoes form from thunderstorms.

For a tornado to form there must be warm, moist air mixing with cool, dry air. When the two air masses meet, instability is created in the atmosphere.

A change in wind direction and an increase in wind speed with increasing height create an invisible, horizontal spinning effect in the lower atmosphere.

The rotating air tilts from horizontal to vertical as air rises. An area of rotation, 2-6 miles wide, then extends through much of the storm.

Tornadoes can form within this area of rotation. A funnel cloud is a spinning vortex extending from the cloud, but it does not reach the ground. A tornado is a funnel that contacts the ground.

Tornadoes are capable of causing massive destruction in a short period of time. Winds in a tornado can reach speeds of up to 300 miles per hour. In an average year, over 800 tornadoes occur in the United States.

Tornadoes can happen at any time of the year and in any climate. Tornadoes have been recorded on every continent with the exception of Antarctica.

Tornado watches are issued when weather conditions are present that can spawn tornadoes. Warnings are issued when a funnel cloud or tornado has been spotted by a trained storm spotter or on weather radar.

If a tornado warning is issued, seek shelter immediately.

Go to a designated tornado shelter, safe room, or the lowest area of your home or building. Remain there until the storm has passed. If you do not have a basement, go to an interior room without windows, such as a bathroom or closet.

You can also seek cover under a sturdy table or desk.

Stay away from windows and doors. Windows could break and doors could blow open putting you at risk of being struck by debris.

If you have time before a storm, bring in or secure any items in your yard that could blow away or cause damage.

If you are in an automobile, get to an indoor shelter. Do not try to out drive the storm. If you are outside with no shelter, go to a low lying area such as a ditch and lie flat.

Cover your head for protection. Do not seek cover under bridges. Stay away from trees or power lines.

If you live in a mobile home, get out and seek cover in a more suitable shelter. Mobile homes can be damaged or destroyed in only a minor tornado.

If possible, either have on sturdy shoes, or have them accessible in your safe room or shelter. Also, try to keep gloves handy.

If there is damage and debris after a tornado, you'll want to protect your feet and hands.

It's also a good idea to cover your mouth and nose. Try to minimize breathing in dust and other contaminants.

This can be done with the use of respirators, or something as simple as a bandana or t-shirt.

Note: In areas served by tornado sirens, you should be aware that they are meant to be heard outdoors. If you are outside when you hear a tornado siren, get inside immediately.

For notification when indoors, your best protection for warnings would be a weather radio, television or regular AM/FM type radio.

Tsunamis

A Tsunami is a series of large waves caused by sudden displacements in the ocean floor (an earthquake), landslides or volcanoes.

These waves can be very large and can submerge coastal cities causing massive destruction and death.

Waves can travel in the open sea at speeds of up to 450 miles per hour. They can reach heights of 100 feet tall. Tsunamis occur most frequently in the Pacific Ocean region, but they can also occur in any large lake, sea or ocean.

Tsunamis are sometimes referred to a "tidal waves", but this is an inaccurate term as tsunamis have nothing to do with tidal movements of the Earth.

If you are in a coastal area when an earthquake occurs or if a tsunami warning is issued, stay calm and get to higher ground as soon as possible. If you cannot get to higher ground, go to the highest floor of building.

Tsunamis are preceded by a rapidly receding tide. The low tide is created by the growing wave further out at sea. If you are on a beach and the tide appears to be receding rapidly, or changing in an untimely pattern, listen for warnings and get to higher ground immediately.

Winter Storms

A winter storm (also known as a Blizzard) forms when two air masses of different temperatures and moisture levels collide. Winter storms usually form when a cold, dry, Arctic air mass moves south and interacts with a warm, moist air mass moving north from the Gulf of Mexico.

Winter storms can cause many problems. Extreme cold, heavy snow and ice are a few of the threats caused by these storms. Reduced visibility, slippery roads and other hazardous conditions can also occur. The best thing to do is stay home unless you absolutely need to leave.

Winter storm watches or warnings may be issued when the threat exists for extreme cold, heavy snow or ice.

Winter storms are usually predictable, so you can prepare for them. Stock up on needed supplies before the storm arrives. Winter storms often knock out power.

Be sure you are prepared to deal with cold temperatures and an extended period of not leaving your home. If you have a fire place, keep an adequate supply of logs. Have your flue and chimney inspected regularly. If you have a furnace, have it checked also to keep it running at peak efficiency.

Consider the use of space heaters to reduce energy costs. Insulate your attic, walls and pipes in your home or business before winter arrives.

Extreme cold can be very hazardous. Wear layered clothing if you'll be exposed to the cold. If temperatures warm up, you can remove clothing items. It is better to be too warm than too cold. Try to limit your exposure to extreme cold.

Gather snow and ice removal equipment in advance. Have a shovel to clear snow and rock salt to melt ice on walkways and stairs.

If traveling through areas where storms are expected, be sure to let others know where you'll be going. Check weather forecasts and try to avoid travelling during the storm.

Carry a cell phone with you and be sure it's charged. Be sure you always know where you are in case you need to call for help.

Always keep your car fueled with at least a half tank of gas. Keep a blanket, tire chains and snow removal equipment (shovel, snow brush and ice scraper) in your car. If your car gets stuck or stranded, stay with it. It can provide temporary shelter from the cold and will make it easier for rescuers to find you.

To signal for help, tie a brightly colored cloth to your antenna or place it in the top of a rolled up window. Turn on your hazard flashers to signal others, but only when your engine is running. Using lights with the engine off will cause your battery to drain.

Have a portable emergency kit with you. Your vehicle emergency kit should be similar to your home kit. Include some water, snacks and a first aid kit. Keep a flashlight or glow sticks in the car so you can have light if needed. It's also a good idea to carry road flares.

Use your engine and heater just long enough to take off the chill in the car. This will help conserve fuel. Have a portable emergency kit with you. Drive with care and allow more time to get where you're going.

Winter driving requires extra attention. Accelerate and decelerate slowly. Be sure to allow further stopping distance on wet or slippery surfaces. You may be the best driver in the world, but unfortunately, not everyone else is.

If you don't need to drive, stay home. The best place to experience a winter storm is from the warmth and comfort of your home.

Wildfires

Wildfires are also known as brush fires, grass fires, forest fires, or wild land fires. They can be caused by natural sources such as lighting igniting dry vegetation. They can also be man-made, caused by arson or unintentionally by vehicles or carelessness.

Areas affected by hot and dry climates are more at risk, though wildfires can occur anywhere. These fires burn millions of acres each year and cause extensive property damage. Many lives have been lost due to wildfires.

On average, 4 out of 5 wildfires are human caused. Fires can spread rapidly, as they are often fueled by strong winds.

You may not be able stop an existing wildfire, but there are some things you can do to minimize your risk.

Allow at least a 30 foot safety zone around your home. This includes clearing dead vegetation, leaves, brush, or fallen trees and branches. Remove any combustible materials from this area. Keep your grass no taller than 2 inches.

Increasing the distance of vegetation from your home will increase your fire safety.

Remove tree limbs within 15 feet of the ground.

Ask your power supplier to remove branches from around power lines.

Trim tree branches and shrubs that are within 15 feet of your chimney or stove pipe.

Stack firewood at least 100 feet from your home.

Store any flammable materials in approved containers away from the house and away from any heat sources.

Keep gas grills and propane tanks at least 15 feet from your house.

Remove debris and vegetation from under decks and porches.

Consider the use of fire resistant siding materials on your home. Materials such as stucco, metal, brick, cement shingles, concrete and rock provide good protection.

Also consider using tile roofing. This is more fire resistant than wood. If remodeling, renovating or considering new construction, use fire resistant materials.

Remove vines or other vegetation from the walls and roof of your house.

Replace highly flammable vegetation in your yard with less flammable species.

Create a second safety space around your home. The second space should start at the 30 foot zone and continue out to 100 feet.

Try to reduce, remove or replace flammable vegetation in this area.

If you have time before you are evacuate, place a hose with a water sprinkler on your roof. Leave the water on to help wet the area.

You can also wet down areas around your home to reduce the spread of fire.

If you are evacuated, do not return to your home or property until told it is safe to do so.

Wildfire Prevention

A wildfire can spread very fast. If you see a small fire, notify the fire department immediately.

Camping is fun, but be sure to make safe fires. Completely extinguish all camp fires before leaving.

You can prevent wildfires by not throwing out lit cigarettes. Also use care when smoking in dry areas. If possible, just don't smoke if there is a high risk of fire!

If using off road vehicles, use a spark arrestor. This will not completely prevent fires, but it will help. Sparks or heat from a vehicle exhaust can ignite fires in dry brush and grass.

Do not use open flame grills during high risk fire times.

If "red flag" warnings are issued, use extreme care with fire. These National Weather Service warnings are usually issued during periods of drought, high winds, and low humidity.

During these times, fires may be banned in certain areas.

Volcanoes

There are more than 1500 active volcanoes on the Earth. 80 or more are found under the ocean waters. Volcanoes are what helped shape our planet. The largest active volcano currently is Mauna Loa in Hawaii. It measures 13,677 feet above sea level.

Over 50% of the most active and dormant volcanoes are found in an area known as the "Ring of Fire". The "Ring of Fire extends along the western northern and eastern perimeter edge of the Pacific Ocean. Nearly 90% of the world's earthquakes and about 81% of the largest earthquakes on Earth occur within the ring.

Volcanoes are dangerous because they can spew burning ash into the atmosphere that can travel for thousands of miles. Flowing lava can destroy anything in its path and falling debris from the eruption can cause additional damage and injuries.

If a volcano is predicted to occur, follow orders issued by authorities. Try to avoid any areas that are downwind of the eruption. Stay out of river valleys and stay downstream of the volcano because mud flows often occur after an eruption.

If you are inside your home or business, close all doors and windows. Be sure to bring in pets and children. If you are outside, seek shelter inside immediately.

If you are outside and there is falling debris, get on the ground and curl up in ball. Cover your head with your hands.

Protect yourself from falling ash by wearing long-sleeved shirts and long pants. Volcanic ash can irritate your eyes and lungs. Wear a dusk mask or respirator and goggles to protect your nose, mouth and eyes. If ash accumulates on your roof, clear it off.

Ash can be heavy and may cause your roof to collapse.

Although there are not many active volcanoes in the United States, there are many locations that have potential to erupt at some time in the future.

Thousands of people visit Yellowstone National Park in northwest Wyoming to see the "Old Faithful" geyser. "Old Faithful" is a regular eruption of boiling water.

What many people don't know is that Yellowstone is on top of what is possibly the largest "super volcano" in the world.

Super volcanoes have the potential to create a massive eruption that could cause extreme destruction and potentially alter the climate of the Earth.

In the state of Hawaii, you can witness the largest and most active volcanoes in the world. The Mauna Loa volcano is the largest on Earth by volume. The Kilauea volcano is the most active.

Volcanoes affect people in locations around the world. Even if you are not near the lava flow or debris, the ash from an eruption can travel thousands of miles.

If you ever encounter volcanic activity, always follow instructions provided by alert warnings. If you are told to evacuate it is in your best interest to do so.

Chapter 7

Man Made Threats

Terrorism

Terrorism is defined as "The use of unlawful violence or threat of unlawful violence to induce fear; intended to coerce or to intimidate governments or societies in the pursuit of goals that are generally political, religious, or ideological." As long as man has been on the earth, there has been terrorism.

There are hundreds of groups around the world who seek to cause change through violent methods. Terrorists seek to cause maximum casualties and damage in the most efficient method possible. This is usually accomplished through the use of explosives. In recent years we have seen an increase in the creativity of terrorists.

Non-traditional methods such as chemical, nuclear and biological attacks have caused new fears, as well as the aircraft attacks of September 11th 2001. The way we go about our day to day lives has been changed because of terrorism.

Terrorists can work in a variety of ways. Some prefer to use psychological terrorism. This creates fear, stress and chaos without actually causing any physical destruction. It is often brought about by intimidation or hoaxes.

Bomb threats are an example of psychological terrorism. Others choose more traditional methods of destruction such as the actual use of explosives or other types of weapons to inflict maximum damage or injury.

Terrorism can happen anywhere, at any time. High risk targets present more of a threat. High risk targets may include places such as government offices, schools, churches, large public gatherings, airports and other transportation facilities.

Terrorists seek opportunities to commit acts. They will often plan attacks months or years in advance.

Terrorists will often scout locations and conduct surveillance. It is not uncommon for terrorists to conduct "test runs" where security will be tested to see if they will be challenged.

Things that may appear strange may be indicators of something more serious.

Things to Look For

Talk of planning an event. You may overhear someone speaking of planning an incident. Notify authorities and provide as much information as possible.

If someone shows an interest in the acquisition of explosives or other bomb making materials, authorities should notified.

Notify authorities if you see someone taking photos, using a video camera, sketching pictures or taking notes in high risk areas.

Inquiries about security procedures, staffing of businesses, location of surveillance cameras or other sensitive questions may be example of probing. Terrorists may be gathering operational information to plot an attack.

Possession or the active seeking of items inconsistent with someone's employment or hobby: Examples of this would include weapons, identification badges, uniforms, equipment, explosives or literature about the building of explosives.

Be aware of people with known associations to fanatical groups or criminal organizations. Someone expressing an active interest in these types of groups should be of concern.

Reporting

If you have concerns about a suspicious act, report it to authorities. If there is an emergency, call 911 immediately.

If it is not urgent, contact the non-emergency number of your local law enforcement authorities. There are some very important things to remember when making a report.

Accuracy is extremely important. If reporting something suspicious, explain why it is out of the ordinary. Tell only the facts about what you see, not opinions. Gather an accurate description of the person and / or vehicle.

When describing a person, use the following information: Race, sex, clothing, hair color, approximate age, height and weight. Look for identifying features such as a mustache or beard, tattoos, scars or disabilities. If you overhear someone, describe how they sound.

Listen for accents, speech impairments or any other identifying traits.

When describing a vehicle, gather the following information: License plate number, color, make and model. Also look for identifying features such as damage, decals or accessories. If the vehicle is moving, describe its direction of travel.

If you think something is not right, report it in a timely manner. Your quick actions and accurate descriptions may save lives.

By being vigilant and reporting suspicious activity we can help to prevent acts of terrorism or other criminal acts.

Bomb Threats

If you have received a threat on the telephone, remain calm. Try to obtain as much information as possible from the caller. If you have caller ID, write down the telephone number.

Try to determine a specific location where the bomb is located and what it looks like. Ask when it will detonate. Ask the caller why they want to do harm. Make a note of the time you received the call. Try to determine if the caller is male or female.

Listen for traits in the voice such as an accent, background noise or if the caller is an adult or child.

Keep the caller on the line as long as possible. Do not hang up on the caller. If another person is with you, have them call 911.

If you are alone, call 911 after the caller disconnects with you. The decision to evacuate will be based on your perceived threat.

Suspicious Packages

Terrorists occasionally have used the mail system or other delivery services to further their criminal acts.

Do not open a suspicious package if you see protruding wires, oily stains, powdery substances felt through an envelope, or if you hear a ticking sound.

Other suspicious indicators may include a package with excessive postage, a poorly typed or badly handwritten address, incorrect spelling of common words, strange return address or mail not addressed to a specific person.

If you receive a suspicious package, do not shake or empty the contents. Put the package down in a secure location.

Do not carry it around to show others, but do alert others in the area of the potential hazard. Minimize your exposure. Do not sniff, taste, touch or examine the contents.

Do not use a cell phone or 2 way radio near the package. Use of these devices can emit signals that may cause explosives to detonate.

If you have handled a package with an unknown residue or powder, wash your hands immediately with soap and water. Notify authorities immediately.

Types of Terrorism

Agro Terrorism: This is the act of tampering with or damaging the food supply through the use malicious use of pathogens to cause disease.

Bio Terrorism: Bio terrorism is the intentional release of germs, biological materials, viruses, bacteria or other agents used to cause death or illness in humans, animals or plants.

Domestic Terrorism: Terrorist acts committed by an American citizen against Americans.

Cyber Terrorism: Cyber terrorists use computer resources to intimidate or coerce others by causing problems.

Criminals may hack into computer networks causing dangerous changes. They can digitally steal funds, information or identities without the owner's knowledge.

As computer technology becomes more common in our society, this problem grows along with it. Prosecution of these crimes is often difficult because the suspects can be spread around the world.

Eco Terrorism: The FBI defines eco terror as the use or threatened use of violence of a criminal nature against people or property by an environmentally oriented, subnational group for environmental or political reasons, or aimed at an audience beyond the target, often of a symbolic nature.

Eco terrorists often target people or businesses who commit cruelty to animals or by damaging the environment through construction or industrialization.

International Terrorism: Acts committed around the globe by various terrorist groups crossing international borders. Attacks are often based on disagreements over foreign policy or beliefs.

Narco Terrorism: Terrorism where there is a connection between drug traffickers and international terrorists. Drug dealers often sell drugs to finance terrorist operations.

State Sponsored Terrorism: Non-military personnel who are committing terrorist acts under the direction of a formal structured national government.

Religious Terrorism: Terrorists who use violence under the theory that the beliefs of their chosen religion are the rule. Anyone who deviates from the group's beliefs should be destroyed.

Workplace / School Violence

Violence at schools and in the workplace should not be taken lightly. Acts of violence at schools and in the workplace can often be considered acts of terrorism. Monitor the behavior of students or employees and watch for abnormal things.

Disgruntled persons often speak freely about bad things they would like to do. Some may only be joking, but all threats need to be addressed, even if they are minor.

Schools and business should have emergency plans in place should an incident occur. Both workplaces and schools should have written policies stating what violence is and that it will not be tolerated.

Remain observant, report all concerns and do all you can to reduce the opportunities for a terrorist to be successful. Staff, students or employees should all be trained on what to do, should violence occur.

If you feel someone may be a potential threat, notify security, a work supervisor or school administrator immediately. You can also notify the police by calling 911.

Be sure to document the incident. If someone is actively showing signs of aggression, remain calm. Try to defuse the situation by calmly reasoning with the person. Good communication skills can often de-escalate situations.

If the anger escalates, or there is an immediate threat to your life, remove yourself from the situation. Do whatever you can to protect yourself. Call for help as soon as you can. If weapons are involved, seek cover or get out of the area.

Do not try to confront an armed person. Schools and businesses should have an evacuation or lock down plan in place should a violent incident occur.

If an employee is terminated in the workplace, extra vigilance should be shown. If your business has security, they should be notified and present during the termination process.

If threats are made, you must take them seriously.

Every school or employer should have plans in place for active shooters or other acts of violence.

Hazardous Materials

Hazardous materials are around us every day. Chemicals are used in many aspects of industrial production. They help to improve our lives but they can also cause havoc if they are used improperly or released accidentally.

Some of the most dangerous chemicals in the world pass through our cities and neighborhoods every day. Trains and trucks passing by our homes, schools, churches, and businesses have the potential to cause major problems because of the hazardous cargo they carry.

These materials can come in the form of explosives, flammable and combustible substances, poisons, and radioactive materials.

Occasionally accidents can occur during industrial production, storage, transportation, use, or disposal of these materials. Your community could be at risk if a chemical is used in an unsafe manner.

Chemicals are sometimes released in harmful amounts into the environment where you live, work, or play. The release may be an accident, or it may be intentional, as hazardous materials are also a point of interest with terrorists.

If there is a release of hazardous chemicals, try to stay away from the source. If you are outside, get as far away as possible from the danger area. Try to stay upstream, uphill, and upwind from the threat. Tell others to move out of the area. Avoid inhaling any gases, fumes and smoke. Cover your mouth with a cloth while evacuating the area.

If you are at home, quickly bring your children and pets inside. Close and lock all exterior doors and windows.

Close all vents, fireplace dampers, and as many interior doors as possible. Turn off air conditioners and ventilation systems. In large buildings, set your ventilation systems to 100 percent recirculation so no outside air is drawn into the building.

If this is not possible, all ventilation systems should be closed or turned off completely.

Shelter in Place

Go into your pre-selected shelter room. This room should be above ground and should have the fewest openings to the outside (Chemicals in the air will sink, so you will be safer in a higher location).

Seal gaps under doorways and windows with wet towels or plastic sheeting and duct tape.

You will also want to seal any gaps around air conditioning units, bathroom and kitchen exhaust fans, and any stove or dryer vents with duct tape and plastic sheeting, wax paper or aluminum wrap. This may help to prevent contaminated air from entering your home. Use material to fill any cracks or holes in the room.

People often have concerns about sealing themselves in the home. This is a valid point as there are hazardous chemicals in the home. Houses are made to ventilate. This prevents the buildup of carbon dioxide.

Ten square feet of floor space per person will provide sufficient air to prevent carbon dioxide build up for up to five hours, assuming normal breathing rates while resting.

However, it is not recommended that you shelter yourself in a sealed room for more than 2-3 hours.

The effectiveness of such sheltering diminishes with time as the carbon dioxide levels build. Contaminated air outside can also gradually seep in, as it not possible to seal every leak in your home.

Evacuation from the area is recommended if a prolonged toxic event is expected.

If you are exposed to gas or vapors that have entered your shelter, take shallow breaths through a cloth or a towel held over your mouth and nose.

Avoid eating or drinking anything that may be contaminated.

Some people choose to have breathing respirators or gas masks in their emergency supply kit. These are available at military surplus stores or other businesses that sell survival supplies.

If you have been exposed to any chemicals, seek medical assistance immediately. If information is available from authorities, follow decontamination instructions.

You may be advised to take a thorough shower, or you may be advised to stay away from water and follow another decontamination method.

Clothing may need to be disposed of. Be sure to place the contaminated items in a tightly sealed container. Do not let the contaminated items come into contact with other items or people.

If you come into contact with other people, tell them you may have been contaminated with a toxic substance. Avoid physical contact until you have been properly decontaminated.

If you witness an accident involving a tanker truck or train, do not approach the vehicle. If you see any spilled liquids, airborne mists, or condensed solid chemical deposits, get as far away as possible, and do not touch or smell them.

Notify authorities of what you see. If you see any victims in the danger area, do not approach or touch them until the hazardous material has been identified. Do not enter contaminated areas without proper personal protective equipment.

In the event of an incident, you may be asked to evacuate. If told to evacuate, do so immediately. Be sure to bring your emergency supply kit with you.

Return home only after you are told it is safe to do so. Stay tuned to a radio or television for information on evacuation routes, temporary shelters, and procedures. Follow only the routes recommended by authorities. Do not take shortcuts as the route may not be safe.

If you have time before you leave, minimize contamination in your home by closing all windows, shutting all air vents, and turning off attic fans.

After the event is over, you should thoroughly ventilate your home or business to remove any residual contamination. Ask local authorities how to properly clean your home or property.

Report any remaining hazards to emergency services personnel.

If hazardous waste is present, it should only be removed by trained professionals.

Check with your local emergency management office to find out what types of hazardous threats are in your area.

Disease Outbreaks / Biological Attacks

Diseases are around us every day. Some diseases can spread rapidly, sometimes turning into a pandemic. A pandemic is an infectious disease outbreak that spreads through human populations across a large region or worldwide.

Recent outbreaks have included the H1N1 virus (also known as Swine Flu), Avian Influenza (Bird Flu) and SARS (Severe Acute Respiratory Syndrome). Though you can't prevent disease outbreaks, you can do some things to minimize the effects.

Be aware of disease warnings. If vaccinations are available, you should consider getting one. Influenza, also known as "the flu" is the most common virus spread among humans. It affects thousands of people each year.

The elderly and young children are the most vulnerable. Flu shots are available year round, but they are often in short supply as flu season nears (late fall).

Symptoms of the flu may include: fever, runny or stuffy nose, chills, headaches or body aches and fatigue.

The best way to prevent the spread of viruses is to limit your exposure to those who are infected. Avoid contact with items handled by those who may be sick. Sanitize things such as telephones, computer keyboards, and toys.

When you are infected, don't share cups, glasses or silverware without properly washing them first. Clean and sanitize bathrooms, door knobs, light switches or anything else that may have been touched.

If you are coughing or sneezing, stay home until you show no symptoms for at least 24 hours.

Most importantly wash your hands with soap and water after shaking hands, or touching items that may be contaminated. If you feel sick, you may want to contact a medical professional.

Biological Agents as Weapons

Biological agents are organisms or toxins that can kill or incapacitate people, livestock, and crops.

Biological agents can be used as weapons. The three basic groups of biological agents that could be used are bacteria, viruses, and toxins. Most biological agents are difficult to grow and maintain.

Many break down quickly when exposed to sunlight and other environmental factors, while others, such as anthrax spores live for a long time. A biological attack may not be immediately obvious. Symptoms may start showing up days or even weeks after a release.

Medical assistance may not be immediately available. The cause of the illness may not be known and it may take time to determine a treatment.

In the event of a known incident, listen to the media for official instructions. If a biological attack were to occur, be sure to follow the instructions provided by the media.

The decision to evacuate or shelter in place will depend on the location and intensity of the attack.

If you encounter an unknown or suspicious substance, you should move away quickly and contact authorities. Seek medical attention if you become ill.

If you come into contact with unknown or suspicious substance, wash with soap and water immediately.

If your clothing or other items are infected, remove them are securely bag them. Seek medical attention for full decontamination.

Pathogen Delivery Methods

Aerosols - Biological agents are dispersed into the air, forming a fine mist that may drift for miles. Inhaling the agent may cause disease in people or animals.

Powders: Spores such as anthrax can be spread through powders. These powders can be inhaled or absorbed through the skin when touched causing illness.

Animals: Some diseases can spread by insects and animals.

Insects can carry disease, which can then infect humans and animals when bitten. You can minimize insect infestation by draining standing water and maintaining a sanitary area. Wear insect repellent or protective clothing when outside in high risk areas.

Food and water contamination: Some pathogenic organisms and toxins may persist in food and water supplies. Most microbes can be killed, and toxins deactivated, by properly cooking food and boiling water.

Most microbes are killed by boiling water for one minute, but some require longer. Keep counter tops clean that are used for food preparation.

Explosives: Toxins may also be spread through the use of explosive dispersion.

Human Contact (person-to-person): This is the easiest way to spread germs. Germs can be spread by physical contact, or airborne methods such as coughing or sneezing.

Avoiding contact with sick people and frequently washing your hands are the best prevention for the spread of germs. Waterless hand sanitizers are also effective.

HEPA Filters

High Efficiency Particulate Air (HEPA) filters are useful tools in biological attacks as well as maintaining the air quality in your home or office. If you have a central heating and cooling system that uses a HEPA filter, leave it on if it is running or turn the fan on if it is not running.

Circulating the air in the house through the filter will help to remove particulates from the air. Portable HEPA filters can be moved into your safe room to help clean the air.

Note: HEPA filters will not filter chemical agents.

CHAPTER 8

What Else Can You Do?

There are many dangers that can be found in your home. To prevent potential problems in your home, here are some tips on simple things you can do to improve safety.

Home Hazards

Repair defective wiring or leaky gas connections.

If you use a fireplace, clean or repair chimneys, flue pipes, vent connections and gas vents.

Secure your water heater by strapping it to wall studs.

Place heavy or large items on lower shelves.

Brace hanging light fixtures.

Do not hang pictures or mirrors near beds.

Store hazardous chemicals such as pesticides, cleaning materials or other dangerous items in a secure location where they are not accessible by children or pets.

Keep the number for Poison Control near your telephone: 1-800-222-1222 (US only).

Fire Safety

Install smoke detectors and clean / test them once a month. Change the batteries at least once a year. Smoke detectors are very inexpensive. Some fire departments will give you one for free and help you with installation.

Keep matches and lighters away from children.

Always have escape routes from your rooms.

Never open doors that are hot. Feel the bottom of the door with your hand. If it is hot, do not open it. Find another way out if your primary exit blocked by fire.

Remember to stay low (crawl) when escaping from fire.

Keep a collapsible escape ladder on upper floors.

Keep a whistle in each bedroom to notify other family members of a fire.

Do not overload electrical outlets.

Place oily rags or waste in covered metal cans.

Consider installing a sprinkler system.

Always store flammable materials in approved containers and keep them away from heat sources.

Keep a working fire extinguisher in your home and teach all members of your family how to use it.

Educate all family members on fire safety.

If there is a fire, get out and stay out. Call 911 from a safe location away from the fire.

Carbon Monoxide

Carbon monoxide is a colorless, tasteless and odorless gas. Exposure can make you very sick, or even cause death.

Improperly vented fuel burning appliances, water heaters, blocked chimney flues and auto exhaust can create a build-up of carbon monoxide.

If you experience persistent headaches, dizziness, ringing in the ears, fatigue, increased perspiration, weakness, nausea or vomiting.

These are all common symptoms of carbon monoxide poisoning. Increased levels of exposure can cause shortness of breath, extreme muscular weakness, convulsions, confusions and unconsciousness.

Severe poisoning can also cause changes in skin color and failure of the heart and lungs.

Prevent exposure to carbon monoxide:

Have your heating systems inspected by a professional. Change or air filters regularly.

Have your chimney and flue inspected and cleaned on a regular basis.

Don't block air intakes around appliances.

Never use a gas range to heat your home. Never operate a gas grill inside your house, or in any enclosed porches or garages.

Never start your car or other fuel burning engine in a closed garage. Always have proper ventilation.

Most importantly, buy a carbon monoxide detector for your home. Be sure to follow the instructions for use provided by the manufacturer.

If you suspect the presence of carbon monoxide in your home, leave the area immediately then, call 911.

Crime Prevention

Not all disasters involve storms or destruction. Some crimes can be a personal disaster if you are a victim. Reduce crime by reducing opportunities for criminals.

Lock your doors and windows when your home or vehicle is unattended. Reduce the temptation for criminals by not leaving items of value in plain sight.

The best crime prevention advice is to use common sense. Report any suspicious activity as soon as you see it. Don't wait for a crime to occur.

You know your home and neighborhood better than the police do. If something doesn't like right, it probably isn't. A proactive response is always better than being reactive.

If you see a crime happening, the best thing to do is to be a good witness. Do not put yourself into situations where you are unsafe or uncomfortable.

Consider taking a self-defense course to protect yourself and to improve your confidence.

Be observant when out in public, don't allow yourself to become a victim of crime. Ask for someone to escort you to your vehicle when you are out alone or if you are in an uncomfortable situation. Always be aware of your surroundings.

Protect your identity. Identity theft is a growing crime that can be a major disaster for you. Do not give out your personal information to unsolicited sources (telemarketers, door to door sales, etc.).

Shred credit card statements, bills and other mail that may contain personal information. If you lose your wallet, checks, or credit cards, notify your bank immediately.

Criminals seek easy opportunities. Do what you can to reduce the chances that you'll be a victim. Contact your local law enforcement agency for more advice on protecting yourself and your property.

Civil Unrest

A growing problem around the world is civil unrest, or rioting. Though many protests are non-violent, some do result in violence and destruction. Disasters often spawn civil unrest and looting.

If you are outside in an area where an incident is occurring, do your best to remove yourself from the situation. Get to a safe location away from the involved area.

If you remain in the area, you run the risk of being arrested or injured, even if you are not involved.

If you are inside a home or building near an incident, stay inside. If possible to do so safely, secure your doors and windows. Try not to draw attention to your-self.

Stay away from doors and windows to protect your-self from rocks, bullets or other projectiles.

Let others know where you are in case you need to be evacuated.

Travel Tips

If you will be travelling on vacation or business, plan ahead. Check news reports and weather forecasts for the area you'll be going. Learn about local hazards and be prepared for them.

If travelling overseas, learn about specific threats such as war zones, high crime areas, or kidnapping dangers. Be sure to learn about local protocol and laws.

If you will be flying, learn what items are prohibited when travelling to expedite your airport security checks.

If you plan to go into the wilderness or remote areas, bring a GPS unit and a cell phone. Be sure to let others know where you'll be going and when you plan to return.

When staying in a hotel, familiarize yourself with the location of emergency exits or tornado shelters. Know where to find the escape route map.

These are usually on the back side of the entry door in a hotel room. Understand warnings that may be used wherever you are. When in doubt, ask hotel staff or local authorities.

If travelling outside of your home country, know how to contact your local embassy should you need assistance in an emergency.

Bring appropriate clothing or supplies for the conditions where you'll be. Try to avoid travelling when conditions may present difficulties.

Always let your family or close friends know your travel plans.

Drive Safely

Driving is one of the most dangerous things we do. Accidents can be frustrating and a great inconvenience. They can also be deadly. Drive carefully all the time, not just during hazardous conditions.

Be courteous to other drivers and always wear your seat belt. It's the law and it can save your life. Do not read or send text messages while driving. It's as dangerous as driving drunk.

Distracted driving can kill you or someone else.

Avoid using a cell phone while driving unless it is an emergency and never read or write texts while driving. Never drive after consuming alcoholic beverages.

Get adequate sleep before driving. Don't try to make a long trip while you are tired. Be well rested so you can get where you're going safely.

Be safe…Arrive alive!

Other Ways to Help

Volunteer. There are many ways for citizens to get involved with disaster planning and response, but the time to get involved is now. Don't wait until a disaster strikes to seek out volunteer opportunities.

If you are not trained ahead of time, you may not be allowed to assist during an incident. There are many excellent groups for you to volunteer your time with, depending on your personal skills and interests.

Learn about the potential threats in your area. Help spread awareness to everyone you know and encourage others to get involved also.

Preparedness is everyone's responsibility. Do your part!

The following pages offer numerous ways you to get involved.

American Red Cross

The American Red Cross is a volunteer organization that has been providing invaluable disaster relief support since 1881.

They assist with food, lodging and other immediate needs during and after a disaster.

In addition to domestic disaster relief, the American Red Cross offers compassionate services in five other areas: community services that help the needy; support and comfort for military members and their families; the collection, processing and distribution of lifesaving blood and blood products; educational programs that promote health and safety such as CPR and first aid classes; and international relief and development programs.

The Red Cross operates nearly 700 locally supported chapters in the United States. Whether it's around the corner or around the world, the Red Cross is there to help. The Red Cross is also the largest supplier of blood and blood products in the United States.

Over four million people donate blood to the Red Cross each year. They collect and distribute roughly half of the blood supply in the United States.

Community Emergency Response Team (CERT)

The CERT program supports local emergency response capabilities by allowing trained volunteers to assist with disasters. This is the modern version of civil defense as it was once known.

CERT teams can provide immediate emergency assistance to victims if other rescuers are not available.

CERT trainings are often presented by local government agencies or other authorized representatives. The classroom training courses provides 20 hours of specialized disaster preparedness instruction.

CERT training educates participants about potential hazards faced in a disaster. Content also includes training on search and rescue, fire safety, disaster medical operations, organizational skills and disaster psychology.

After completing CERT training, participants are encouraged to get involved with community events and training activities that support emergency preparedness.

Citizen Corps

Citizen Corps is a federal program that provides opportunities for people across the country to participate in a wide range of activities to make their families, homes, and communities safer.

Through public education, training opportunities, and volunteer programs, "every American can do their part to be better prepared and better protected and to help their communities do the same".

Citizen Corps is managed at the local level by Citizen Corps Councils, which bring together leaders from law enforcement, fire, emergency medical and other emergency management, volunteer organizations, local elected officials, the private sector, and other community stakeholders.

These Citizen Corps Councils organize public education on disaster mitigation and preparedness, citizen training, and volunteer programs to give people of all ages and backgrounds the opportunity to support emergency services in their community and to safeguard themselves and their property.

Federal Emergency Management Agency (FEMA)

From historical disaster data to training opportunities and everything else within the four basic concepts of emergency management, FEMA offers a variety of training and support resources for citizens.

If you wish to further your education about disasters, FEMA offers free online independent study courses through the Emergency Management Institute and on site courses available at various locations around the US.

You can also learn everything you ever wanted to know about disasters and disaster recovery.

Medical Reserve Corps

If you have experience and skills as a nurse, doctor or other form of medical professional, you can sign up for the Medical Reserve Corps. This is an organization of professionals who are ready to respond to disasters to provide medical assistance.

Specific skills are needed to participate with this organization and travel is often required.

National Fire Corps

Fire Corps volunteers assist local fire and emergency service departments with administrative duties, special programs and life safety education and other services.

Radio Amateur Civil Emergency Service (RACES)

RACES volunteers are trained amateur radio operators. They offer emergency communications services that can called upon in times of need. This is a vital service that utilizes amateur radio frequencies.

In a major disaster, this may be the only communications available. To find out more about how you can get involved with RACES, contact your local emergency management office.

Volunteer Fire Fighting

There are many fire departments across the nation that offer volunteer firefighting opportunities. Training is usually provided by the department, but you can also receive certifications at local community colleges.

Volunteers in Police Service

The demands on law enforcement agencies have increased dramatically in recent years. With budgets being cut further than ever, staffing resources are limited.

At a time when police agencies need every available certified officer on patrol, resources can be stretched thin.

Volunteers can work with a law enforcement agency in a variety of roles. Tasks may include serving as an extra pair of eyes and ears on the street, search and rescue, administrative duties, or other services based on your skills.

You can also serve part time as a reserve or auxiliary officer if you meet certain qualifications. Contact your local law enforcement agency for more information to see what programs are offered.

Other Groups

There are also many private and faith based organizations that provide disaster relief services. Check your local churches and community service groups to find out who offers these services and how you can get involved.

If you have an interest in extreme weather, becoming a storm spotter or storm chaser may be of interest to you. To find out more about how to become certified as storm spotter, contact your local emergency management office or the National Weather Service office in your area.

Courses are usually free and are offered several times a year. You can also find information on the internet or at your local library.

Once trained, you can become a vital part of the community safety team, seeking out severe weather when watches are issued.

Neighborhood Watch

Organize or get involved with a neighborhood watch group.

The police can't be everywhere, so more eyes and ears in your neighborhood can increase safety. Neighborhood Watch is a great way to help make your community a better place to live.

You'll get to know your neighbors and you can help to reduce crime. Contact your local law enforcement agency for more information.

Stay Informed

Monitor news and weather reports. Be aware of current events and potential hazards.

Educate Others

Talk with your friends, family and neighbors. Encourage your church, school, business, or civic organization to host a seminar on safety and emergency planning.

Do everything you to prepare so when something does happen you will be ready!

Chapter 9

Historical Disasters

In order to prepare for the future, you must learn from the past.

History has shown that no location, culture or people are immune from disaster. We can hope a major catastrophe will never happen again, but the unfortunate reality is that something will happen.

Just because something has not occurred where you live or work doesn't mean that it won't. Complacency can kill. We all need to be ready for whatever comes our way.

Whether it's a terrorist attack, a severe weather event or a disease outbreak, everyone should be prepared for the unexpected. There is no need to live in fear, but awareness will only serve to increase your preparedness and safety.

Although there have been thousands of known disasters throughout history, some have gathered more attention than others because of the extreme level of catastrophe.

The following time line demonstrates how disasters can change the way we live our lives. The intent of the list is to show the frequency of incidents and how they can happen anywhere.

This list presents only a small fraction of the lives lost in recent history during "high profile" events. It does not include acts of war and it does not include every disaster for each year listed, as hundreds of disasters occur every year.

There have been many, many more natural and human caused incidents than those listed here. The lessons of our past should serve as a warning for our future.

Remember: It's a matter of *if* a disaster will strike, but *when*…

2018 – Florida: Hurricane Michael, a category 4 storm made landfall leaving severe damage and flooding across the Florida panhandle, parts of Georgia and Alabama as well as leaving millions without power. 6 people were killed with many others injured.

2018 – Indonesia: A 7.5 magnitude earthquake and resulting tsunami struck the island killing more than 840 people.

2018 – North Carolina: Hurricane Florence dumped more than 40 inches of rain in the Carolinas in a 24 hour period as it came ashore causing major flooding in the Carolinas. More than 40 people lost their lives.

2018 – California: More than 12,000 firefighters battled one of the largest wild fires in the state's history. An estimated 300,000 acres were destroyed, including hundreds of homes. 6 lives were lost.

2018 – Parkland, Florida: 17 people lost their lives with 14 others injured after a school shooting at Marjorie Douglas High School.

2017 – Puerto Rico: Hurricane Maria, a category 4 storm, caused massive damage to the island causing a humanitarian crisis. The death toll is not fully known but was estimated to be between 100 and 4,000.

2017 – Las Vegas, Nevada: A sniper opened fire on a crowd attending a country music concert killing 60 and injuring 300 others.

2017 - Sutherland Springs, Texas: A heavily armed shooter killed 26 people, wounding 20 at a church before later killing himself.

2017 – Florida: Hurricane Irma, category 4 storm, knocked out power to nearly eight million homes, leaving more than 130 dead. At the time it was the strongest hurricane the hit the US since Hurricane Katrina in 2005.

2017 – Texas: Hurricane Harvey left several feet of rain which flooded southeast Texas (Houston) and surrounding areas. The storm caused the most flooding since Hurricane Katrina in 2005. More than 100 people died.

2016 – Orlando, Florida: An ISIS inspired shooter killed 49 people, injuring more than 50 in a nightclub.

2015 – Philadelphia, Pennsylvania: An AMTRAK train derailed, killing 8, injuring more than 200.

2015 – San Bernardino, California: Terrorists attacked a facility killing 14 and seriously injuring 22 others.

2014 – US East Coast: A massive winter storm killed 22 people and knocked out power for days, affecting upwards of 1.2million homes and businesses. Power was not restored for up to 2 weeks in some locations.

2014 - Zhaotong, China: A 6.5 magnitude earthquake destroyed or damaged 155,000 homes, displacing nearly 230,000 people. The death toll was over 600 with thousands more injured.

2013 – Boston, Massachusetts – Two pressure cooker bombs exploded near the finish line of the Boston Marathon, killing 3 people, injuring more than 260 others.

2013 – Colorado: Large portions of the state were ravaged by forest fires. 2 people were killed and nearly 600 structures were destroyed. Not long after the fires, the state was soaked with torrential rains causing widespread flooding across 17 counties. Thousands of residents were displaced and at least 8 people killed. Nearly 20,000 homes were damaged or destroyed.

2013 – Moore Oklahoma: An EF5 tornado touched down for 37 minutes over a 17 mile path killing more than 55 people.

2012 – Newtown, Connecticut: A shooter killed 28 people at Sandy Hook elementary school.

2012 – US East Coast: Superstorm Sandy was a massive storm which affected 24 states from Florida to Maine. More than 230 people were killed as a result of the storm. The damage costs were estimated at over 70 million dollars. The storm was the largest Atlantic hurricane ever recorded when it made landfall.

2011 – Joplin Missouri: An EF-5 tornado tore through the city center causing extensive damage. More than 160 deaths occurred with nearly 1,000 people injured. This storm added to the already high 2011 death toll, making this one of the deadliest severe weather years in US history.

2011- Tuscaloosa Alabama: An EF-4 tornado hit the heart of the city causing over 2 Billion dollars in damage. At least 281 people were killed and thousands more injured as storms ripped through 6 southern states.

2011 – Japan: A magnitude 9.0 earthquake caused massive damage along the east coast of Japan's main island. A resulting tsunami caused even more damage and death when it hit the coast. The combined incident caused an international nuclear scare when a nuclear reactor complex was severely damaged. More than 15,000 people were killed.

2010 - Haiti: Exact casualties resulting from a magnitude 7 quake are still unknown, but an estimated 200,000 + people are believed to have been killed.

2010 – Iceland: A volcanic eruption disrupted air travel around the world due to a massive ash cloud.

2009 – Fort Hood, Texas: 13 people were killed and 30 more were wounded during a shooting rampage.

2009 – Oklahoma: A series a tornadoes tore through the state killing 8 people, injuring a dozen more.

2008 – Sichuan China: A magnitude 8 earthquake killed nearly 70,000 people and left more than 374,000 injured. Over 4.8 million people were left homeless.

2008 – Virginia: Tornadoes struck the Norfolk area injuring over 200 people. More than 140 homes were destroyed.

2008 – New England: An ice storm left 800,000 people without electricity for several days.

2007 – Midwest & Northeast US: A massive January winter storm moved across 9 states causing 65 storm related deaths and extensive power outages.

2007 – Louisville, Kentucky: A freight train carrying hazardous chemicals derailed and burned causing a major evacuation. A 20 mile stretch of Interstate 65 was closed.

2007 – Greensburg, Kansas: An EF5 tornado that measured almost 2 miles wide destroyed 95% of the town. 11 People died with many others injured. In what proved to be a test of determination, the town rebuilt as a new "green" environmentally friendly city, improving the quality of life for all who chose to remain there.

2007 – California: 24 wildfires over a one week period killed 7 people and injured nearly 90 others. The fires burned over 516,000 acres, causing more than 500,000 residents to be evacuated.

2007– Blacksburg, Virginia: A student killed 32 people on the University of Virginia campus during a shooting rampage.

2006 – Texas: In a 4 month period, wildfires burned more than 3.9 million acres. An estimated 400 homes were destroyed. More than 10,000 horses and cattle were killed as well as 11 people.

2006 – Hawaii: A dam collapsed sending 300 million gallons of water into the valley below. Seven people were killed.

2005 – Pakistan: A 7.6 magnitude earthquake killed over 40,000 people and caused major damage to structures.

2005 – Louisiana / Mississippi: More than 1,800 people were killed by Hurricane Katrina as it flooded the US Gulf Coast. Southern Louisiana was the area hardest hit. It was one of the worst hurricanes in US history. Property damage was estimated at over $81 billion dollars.

2004 - Indian Ocean: A tsunami caused by a 9.3 magnitude earthquake killed more than 225,000 people as it came ashore in Indonesia, Sri Lanka, India and Thailand. The earthquake had the longest faulting ever observed at the time, lasting between 8 and 10 minutes. It is one of the largest quakes ever observed on a seismograph. Resulting earthquakes were triggered as far away as Alaska.

2004 – Beslan, Russia: Terrorists took over a school and held 1,100 people hostage. During the incident and attempted rescue, the terrorists set off bombs and engaged in a shootout killing 334 hostages.

2003 – Southern California: Wildfires consumed more than 800,000 acres and killed 22 people.

2003 – Worldwide: SARS (Severe Acute Respiratory Syndrome), a deadly strain of pneumonia, was responsible for nearly 400 deaths worldwide.

2003 – West Warwick, Rhode Island: A fire caused by a pyrotechnics display caused a fire in a nightclub during a rock concert. 100 people were killed and 150 were injured.

2002 – Central & Southeast US: A series of 70 tornadoes destroyed homes and buildings across 14 states. 36 people were killed by the storms.

2002 – Virginia / West Virginia: A massive rain storm dumped about 6 inches of rain in 4 hours, causing major landslides and flooding. At least a dozen people died and nearly 2,000 homes and businesses were destroyed.

2001 – New York City: 19 terrorists hijacked 4 commercial airplanes loaded with passengers. Two of the hijacked airplanes intentionally flew into the World Trade Center buildings, causing them to collapse. At about the same time, a third airplane was intentionally crashed into the Pentagon building in Arlington, Virginia. A fourth aircraft crashed in a field near Shanksville Pennsylvania. It is believed the fourth plane was headed to the White House in Washington DC. 2,995 people were killed and more than 6,000 injured during these attacks. These events were a major turning point in American homeland security.

1998 – Central America: Hurricane Mitch, one of the most powerful hurricanes in history, killed nearly 11,000 people, causing massive damage.

1997 – Central Texas: Tornadoes caused 29 deaths, 32 injuries and an estimated $20 million in damage.

1996 – Northeast US: A massive blizzard dumped huge amounts of snow causing extensive problems. Resulting floods from melting snow caused more problems. An estimated 154 people died as a result of the blizzard, with more deaths resulting from the flooding. The storm caused over $3 billion in damage.

1995 – Oklahoma City, Oklahoma: The Alfred P. Murrah Federal building was destroyed when a truck filled with explosives detonated. 168 people were killed in the blast.

1993 - New York City: A terrorist attempted to blow up the World Trade Center but failed. Despite the failure to collapse the buildings, 6 people are killed and over 1,000 were injured.

1992 - Hurricane Andrew (a category 5 storm) killed 26 people as it came ashore in south Florida and the Gulf Coast. Property damage was estimated at $25 billion. This was the most expensive natural disaster in U.S. history at the time.

1991 – Oakland, California: A wildfire killed 25 people and destroyed over 1,200 acres.

1989 - Loma Prieta California: An earthquake registering 6.9 on the Richter scale caused major damage in San Francisco and surrounding areas.

1988 – USA: An extended drought destroyed crops and fueled wildfires across the west. An estimated 5,000 – 10,000 people were believed to have died from heat related complications.

1986 – Ukraine: An explosion and fire in one of the Chernobyl nuclear reactors released radioactive material that spread over Russia and Europe. 31 people were said to have been killed and thousands more have had illnesses related to the incident.

1985 - Nevado Del Ruiz, Columbia: A volcano killed 25,000 people, most from a resulting mud flow.

1985 – Japan: A 747 airplane crashed into a mountain killing the 520 passengers and crew.

1984 – Bhopal, India: A pesticide plant released toxic gas into the atmosphere. The death toll varies, but it is believed to be between 2,000 and 16,000. A 2006 report stated there were over 558,000 people injured.

1980 – USA: A prolonged drought with excessive heat is believed to have killed over 10,000 people.

1980 – Mount St. Helens, Washington: A volcano erupted killing 57 people and destroyed more than 200 homes.

1976 – Tangshan, China: A magnitude 8 earthquake killed somewhere between 255,000 and 655,000 people.

1975 – Ru River, China: 230,000 people were killed when the Banqiao Dam collapsed. Massive flooding resulted.

1970 – Bangladesh: A hurricane and resulting floods killed between 500,000 – 1,000,000 people.

1969 – Mississippi: Hurricane Camille, a Category 5 storm came ashore with winds in excess of 190 miles per hour.

1966 – Austin, Texas: A gunman at the University of Texas went on a shooting rampage killing 16 and wounding 31 others.

1962 – Tokyo, Japan: A freight train collided with a commuter train killing 163 and injuring 400.

1953 – Waco, Texas: A tornado destroyed more than 850 homes and killed 114 people.

1950 – Eastern US: A massive winter storm crippled the east coast. 353 people were believed to be killed as a result of the storm.

1947: Texas City, TX: A ship carrying munitions exploded in port causing a fire that destroyed much of the city. 516 people were killed.

1940 – Midwest US: A blizzard killed 154 people as it took many by surprise with heavy snow and extreme cold.

1933 – Long Beach, California: A 6.3 magnitude earthquake killed 115 people.

1928 – Florida: A hurricane with 140+ mph winds killed more than 2,500 people as it came ashore.

1927 – Bath, Michigan: An angry school board member blew up a school. 45 people were killed and 58 injured. Most of the victims were students.

1925 – Illinois, Indiana & Missouri: A massive tornado destroyed homes and killed nearly 700 people as it tracked across the three states.

1918 – An outbreak of Spanish Influenza killed over 500,000 people in the United States.

1912 – North Atlantic Ocean: 1,517 passengers died when the Titanic sank after striking an iceberg. The Titanic was the largest passenger ship in the world at the time. It was thought to be unsinkable.

1906 – San Francisco, California: An earthquake caused fires that burned for 4 days. More than 500 city blocks were destroyed, leaving 225,000 people homeless. An estimated 3,000 lives were lost.

1904 – Eden, Colorado: A train derailed on a bridge during a flash flood. 96 people were killed.

1902 – Mt. Pelee, West Indies: A volcanic eruption destroyed the city of St. Pierre and killed an estimated 40,000 people.

1900 – Galveston, Texas: More than 8,000 were killed when a hurricane submerged the island.

1889 /1890 – Russia: The Asiatic Flu killed more than 250,000 people in Europe alone. The disease also spread through South America, India and Australia with a high mortality rate.

1889 – Johnstown, Pennsylvania: The town was flooded when the South Fork Dam burst. Over 2,200 were killed as 1,600 homes were washed away.

1883 – Mt. Krakatoa, Indonesia: A volcano and subsequent tsunami killed more than 36,000 people.

1881 – Vietnam: A hurricane killed an estimated 300,000 people.

1881 – Chatsworth, Illinois: 81 people were killed and 372 injured when a burning trestle collapsed as a train passed over it.

1871 – Illinois: The "Great Chicago Fire" destroyed the business district of the city.

1871 – Wisconsin: A massive fire that occurred at the same time as the Great Chicago fire destroyed 12 towns and left nearly 1,200 people dead.

1865 – Memphis, Tennessee: More than 1,500 people died when the Sultana, a river boat, sank in the Mississippi River after a boiler exploded on board.

1840 – Natchez, Mississippi: 317 people were killed when a tornado struck. Death counts are believed to be higher because slaves were not counted.

1816 – Mt. Tambora, India: An estimated 92,000 people were killed by a volcanic eruption and related causes.

1811-12 – Missouri: Three of the strongest earthquakes in US history struck the southeast part of the state. Believed to have an estimated magnitude of 7.8 or higher, shaking was felt as far away as New York and Boston.

1806 – Portsmouth New Hampshire: On Christmas Eve the city suffered a major fire.

1802 – Portsmouth, New Hampshire: A Christmas day fire destroyed 132 buildings.

1792 – Mt. Unzen, Japan – A volcanic eruption caused an avalanche that created a tsunami killing 12,000 – 15,000 people in nearby towns.

1780 – Caribbean: A hurricane killed an estimated 20,000 as the storm hit the islands of Barbados and Martinique.

1737 – India: An estimated 300,000 were killed when an earthquake induced typhoon struck Calcutta.

1556 – China: An earthquake is believed to have killed 830,000 people.

1348 – The Bubonic Plague, also known as the Black Death pandemic killed an estimated 75 million people, wiping out 30 to 60 percent of Europe's population.

1287 – The Netherlands: 50,000 people were killed when a seawall on the Zuider Zee failed.

1138 – Syria: A strong earthquake killed about 230,000 people. It is believed to be the fourth deadliest earthquake of all time.

541 – Mediterranean region: A disease believed to be similar to the Bubonic Plague killed an estimated one quarter of the Byzantine population. The exact death toll is not known.

526 – A massive earthquake struck the area currently known as Syria. The quake is believed to have killed 250,000 people.

365 – An earthquake in the Mediterranean Sea destroyed nearly all the towns on the island of Crete. A resulting tsunami affected Alexandria Egypt and other nearby areas. Thousands of people are thought to have been killed.

165 – 180 – Rome: Believed to be small pox or a measles pandemic, 5,000,000 people are believed to have died in what was known as the Antonine Plague, or the Plague of Galen.

79 – Mt. Vesuvius, Italy: A volcano erupted destroying the towns of Pompeii and Herculaneum. More than 10,000 were killed.

It could happen to you…
When the next disaster strikes, will you be ready?

Chapter 10

Disaster Terminology

To better understand a disaster, you should know the terminology. You may have heard some of these terms used while watching the news or listening to warnings.

Each term has definitions included.

Accumulation - The actual measurable depth of any precipitation on the ground during a given time period.

Advisory - Issued by the National Weather Service to highlight weather conditions that require caution, but are not thought to be immediately life threatening.

Al Qaeda – A terrorist organization that opposes non-Islamic governments.

Air Pollution – Chemicals or substances in the atmosphere that are directly or indirectly harmful to living things.

Air Pressure - Weight of the air pressing down on the Earth. It is also known as barometric pressure.

Anemometer - A weather instrument used to measure wind speed.

Arctic Air - Air masses that originate over Canada bringing cold temperatures south.

Atmosphere - A layer of gases surrounding a planet. The Earth's atmosphere is divided into five layers: exosphere, thermosphere, mesosphere, stratosphere, and troposphere.

Aurora Borealis - Often called the "Northern Lights", they occur when energetic particles from a solar storm cause the gases in the upper atmosphere to glow.

Avalanche - A large body of snow, ice or rock and debris sliding down a mountain or hillside.

Barometer - An instrument that measures air pressure.

Barometric Pressure - The pressure exerted by the atmosphere, also known as air pressure.

Beaufort Wind Scale - A system of estimating and reporting wind speeds. It is based on the Beaufort Force or Number, which is composed of the wind speed, a descriptive term, and the visible effects upon land objects and/or sea surfaces. The scale was devised by Sir Francis Beaufort (1777-1857), a hydrographer and officer for the British Royal Navy.

Bermuda High - It's a weather system that often dominates the eastern United States during the summer. A semi-permanent subtropical high-pressure system over the North Atlantic Ocean brings in warm and humid air for many days or weeks at a time. It gets its name because it is sometimes centered near Bermuda. It contributes to U.S. heat waves when it extends west into the Gulf of Mexico and across the Deep South.

Blizzard - An intense winter storm with winds of 35 mph or higher with falling and/or blowing snow that reduces visibility to below 1/4 mile for at least three hours. Blizzards can also have extremely cold temperatures.

Blowing Snow Advisory - When wind driven snow reduces surface visibility, it can cause dangerous driving conditions. Blowing snow may be falling snow or snow that has already accumulated on the ground but is picked up and blown by strong winds.

Breeze - A light wind.

Car Bomb – A vehicle filled with explosives.

Ceiling - The height of the lowest layer of broken or overcast cloud layer.

CIA – Abbreviation for the Central Intelligence Agency.

Climate - The average weather conditions in a certain place or during a certain season.

Clouds - A visible collection of water or frozen ice crystals suspended in the air above the surface.

Coastal Flooding - When winds and/or tides create a rise in the sea level that causes flooding in coastal areas.

Coastal Flood Warning - Land areas along the coast are expected to become, or have become, inundated by sea water above the typical tide action.

Coastal Flood Watch - The possibility exists for the inundation of land areas along the coast within the next 12 to 36 hours.

Cold Front - A boundary between two air masses, one cold and the other warm, moving so that the colder air replaces the warmer air.

Condensation - The change of water vapor to liquid water, as when fog or dew forms.

Coriolis Force - A force that deflects moving objects to one side because of the Earth's rotation.

Cumulonimbus Clouds - A dense and vertically developed cloud that produces thunderstorms. The cloud can bring heavy showers, hail, lightning, high winds and sometimes tornadoes.

Cumulus Clouds – Large, towering fluffy clouds

Cyclone - A term variously applied to tornadoes, waterspouts, dust storms and hurricanes.

Dense Fog - Fog that reduces horizontal visibility to 1/4 mile or less.

Dense Fog Advisory - Issued when dense fog covers a widespread area and reduces visibility to ¼ of a mile or less.

Dew - Water that forms on objects close to the ground when its temperature falls below the dew point of the surface air.

Dew Point - The temperature at which water starts to condense out of a particular air mass. The dew point temperature changes only when the moisture content of the air changes. The higher the dew point, the greater the moisture content is in the air.

DHS – Abbreviation for the Department of Homeland Security, a federal agency tasked with protecting the United States against terrorism.

Dirty Bomb – A conventional explosive device created with radioactive material.

Disturbance - A low pressure system, a tropical area of storminess, or any area in which the weather is in a state of cloudiness, precipitation or wind.

Downburst - A strong downward rush of air, which produces a blast of damaging winds on or close to the surface.

Drizzle - Light rain consisting of water droplets that are very small.

Drought - An extended period of no rainfall.

Dust Devil - Small whirlwinds of dust that form in dry areas such as deserts. They are caused by swirling winds that rise with the warm air found over the ground.

Earthquake - The shaking or movement of a portion of the Earth's surface caused by fault movement.

El Niño - The unusual warming of the surface waters of the eastern tropical Pacific Ocean. It causes changes in wind patterns that have major effects on weather all across the globe. It is the opposite of La Niña.

EMS – Abbreviation for Emergency Medical Service

EMT – Abbreviation for Emergency Medical Technician

Enhanced Fujita Scale – A scale used to measure the intensity of tornadoes based on the amount damage caused.

Also see Fujita Scale. Scale is based on wind speed/damage.

EF-0: Winds 65 - 85 mph
EF-1: Winds 86 - 109 mph
EF-2: Winds: 110 - 137 mph
EF-3: Winds 138 – 167 mph
EF-4: Winds 168 – 199 mph
EF-5: Winds 200 – 234 mph

Environment - The surroundings of a person, place or thing.

EOD – Abbreviation for Explosive Ordinance Disposal, another name for a police, fire or military "bomb squad". EOD teams assist with the removal and disposal of explosive devices.

Erosion - The wearing away of the Earth's surface by the action of moving water, ice, precipitation or wind.

Evaporation - The process of a liquid changing to a vapor.

Excessive Heat Warning - Issued within 12 hours of the onset of the heat conditions listed in the excessive heat watch.

Excessive Heat Watch - Issued when the following conditions occur within 12-36 hours: a heat index of at least 105 degrees for more than 3 hours per day for 2 consecutive days or a heat index more than 115 degrees for any period of time.

Fahrenheit – The scale most commonly used for weather temperature measurement in the United States. It is abbreviated as °F. Using the Fahrenheit scale, the freezing point of water is 32°F and the boiling point is 212°F.

Fallout – Radioactive particles falling from the sky after a radiological release.

Fault - A planar fracture or discontinuity in a volume of rock across which there has been significant displacement. The movement of faults in the ground causes earthquakes.

Farmer's Almanac - A calendar that lists tide data, gives   the positions of the stars and forecasts weather for a year in advance.

FBI – Abbreviation for the Federal Bureau of Investigation,   a US agency tasked with domestic law enforcement.

FEMA – Abbreviation for the Federal Emergency Management Agency

Flash Flood - A rapid and extreme flow of high water into a normally dry area, or a rapid water level rise in a stream or creek above a predetermined flood level, beginning within six hours of a weather event.

Flash Flood Watch - Issued when conditions exist that could cause rapid flooding in low lying areas or in locations where the ground is already saturated from recent rains.

Flash Flood Warning - Issued when rapid flooding is in progress or is imminent in watch areas.

Flood – An expanse of water that submerges land.

Flood Plain – Flat areas bordering rivers or streams that experience periodic or occasional flooding.

Flood Stage - The level at which a stream, river or other body of water will begin to overflow its banks.

Fog - A cloud on the ground that reduces visibility.

Freeze - When temperatures fall below 32 degrees for an extended period of time.

Freeze Warning - Issued when temperatures are expected to fall below 32 degrees for an extended period of time.

Freezing Rain - Rain that falls in liquid form but freezes upon impact to form a coating of glaze on surfaces.

Front - A boundary between two different air masses, resulting in stormy weather. A front usually is a line of separation between warm and cold air masses.

Frost - Formed when solid surfaces are cooled to below the dew point of the surrounding air and below the freezing point of water.

Frost Advisory - Issued when a widespread frost is expected over an extensive area.

Frostbite – A damaging medical condition that occurs when skin is exposed to excessive cold.

F Scale – See Fujita scale

Fujita Scale - The traditional scale used to measure the strength of tornadoes based upon wind speed. The scale ranges from F0 (lowest) to F5 (highest).

F0: winds 40-72 mph - (Light damage)
Branches can be broken off trees.

F1: winds 73-112 mph - (Moderate damage)
Trees snap and mobile home can be pushed off foundations.

F2: winds 113-157 mph - (Considerable damage)
Mobile homes demolished and trees uprooted.

F3: winds 158-206 mph - (Severe damage)
Trains can be overturned and cars lifted off the ground.

F4: winds 207-260 mph - (Devastating damage)
Houses leveled and cars thrown some distance.

F5: winds 261-318 mph - (Incredible damage)
Houses may be lifted and thrown some distance.

Note: Meteorologists are now often using the **Enhanced Fujita** scale measurement.

Funnel Cloud – A rotating column of air extending downward from the base of a cumulonimbus or thunderstorm cloud, not making contact with the ground.

Glacier - A large mass of ice that moves over land.

Glaze - A coating of ice, usually clear and smooth, formed on exposed objects by the freezing of rain, drizzle, or fog.

Global Warming - The theory that increased concentrations of greenhouse gases are causing the surface temperature of the Earth to rise.

Gulf Stream - A warm swift current in the Atlantic Ocean that flows from the Gulf of Mexico along the eastern coast of the United States northeast toward Europe.

Hail – Rain drops inside cumulonimbus clouds are forced upward in the cloud by updrafts, gathering moisture as they rise. As layers of ice form, they will become heavy and will fall from the sky in the form of balls other irregular shapes known as hail stones.

Hard Freeze -When the air temperature is expected to be 26 degrees or colder for at least 4 consecutive hours.

Haze - Tiny particles of dust, smoke, salt or pollution droplets that are scattered through the air.

Haz-Mat – Abbreviation for Hazardous Materials

Heat Advisory - Issued within 12 hours of the onset of the following conditions: a heat index of at least 105 degrees but less than 115 degrees for less than 3 hours per day or if nighttime lows remain above 80 degrees for 2 consecutive days.

Heat Index - The "feel like" temperature on a hot day when you combine humidity with the actual air temperature.

Heat Lightning - Heat lightning is just lightning that is too far away for its thunder to be heard.

Heavy Snow Warning - Issued when snowfall totaling 6 inches or more in 12 hours or less is expected. Also issued when there is 8 inches or more of snow expected in 24 hours or less.

High Pressure System - Mass of warm, dry air that generally brings nice weather.

High Wind Warning - Issued when winds of 40 mph or greater are occurring or expected to occur for at least one hour. It also occurs if winds of 58 mph or greater are expected.

High Wind Watch - Issued when conditions are favorable of the development of high winds.

Humidity - The amount of water vapor in the air.

Hurricane - Intense storms with swirling winds up to 150 mph. usually around 300 miles across, hurricanes are 1,000-5,000 times larger than tornadoes.

Hurricane Season - The six-month period from June 1 to Nov. 30, when conditions are favorable for hurricane development.

Hygrometer - An instrument that measures humidity.

Ice - Water in a solid phase. Water becomes ice when it is cooled below 32 degrees (F) or 0 degrees(C).

Iceberg – A chunk of freshwater ice that has broken off a glacier and is floating in open water.

Ice Storms - They occur when temperatures below a rain cloud are very cold, causing the raindrops to become super cooled (less than 32 degrees Fahrenheit).

Ice Storm Warning - Issued when damaging accumulations of ice are expected during a freezing rain event.

ICS – Incident Command System

IED – Abbreviation for an Improvised Explosive Device.

Indian Summer – Warm weather in the autumn.

Inversion - A layer in the atmosphere where the temperature increases with height.

Jet Stream - A strong high level wind found in the atmosphere that can reach speeds in excess of 200 mph, usually occurring 6 to 9 miles above the ground. These winds often steer the movement of surface air masses and weather systems.

La Niña - A widespread cooling of the surface waters of the eastern tropical Pacific Ocean. It's the opposite of El Niño.

Lake Effect Snow - Localized snow that forms on the downwind side of large lakes. It's common in the late fall and winter in the Great Lakes region when cold, dry air picks up moisture from the unfrozen lake surfaces.

Lightning – An atmospheric discharge of electricity produced during thunderstorms.

Low Pressure System - A cool dry air mass that often brings cooler weather, and storms.

Macroburst - A large down draft of air with an outflow diameter of at least 2.5 miles and damaging winds lasting about 5 to 20 minutes.

Microburst - A small downdraft of air with an outflow diameter of less than 2.5 miles with peak winds lasting from 2 to 5 minutes.

Meteor – Sometimes called a "shooting star", it is a rock made of composite material falling from space.

Meteor Shower - When hundreds of meteors can be seen in the sky at the same time.

Meteorite - A meteor that reaches the Earth's surface.

Meteorologist - A scientist who studies and predicts the weather.

Meteorology - The study of the atmosphere and all its phenomena, including weather and how to forecast it.

Mist – Very small water droplets floating in the air.

MPH – Abbreviation for Miles per Hour, a measure of speed.

Monsoon - A seasonal wind, occurring in Asia that reverses direction between summer and winter. It often brings heavy rains. It also refers to heavy seasonal rains in the southwest United States.

Muggy - The description of warm and humid air.

National Hurricane Center - They issue watches, warnings, forecasts, and analyses of hazardous tropical weather.

National Weather Service – The federal agency that provides climate forecasts and weather warnings for the United States.

Nexrad – Abbreviation for the "NEXt generation weather RADar", a nationwide network of 120 Doppler radars used by the National Weather Service to monitor weather conditions.

NIMS – Abbreviation for the National Incident Management System, a US national emergency response plan.

Nor'easter - A powerful low-pressure system that moves along the Atlantic Coast. It's called a Nor'easter because the coastal winds come from the northeast. Heavy rain, snow and high tides often occur.

Overcast - Widespread layers of clouds covering the sky.

Ozone - Ozone is a form of oxygen that heats the upper atmosphere by absorbing ultraviolet light from sunlight. In the troposphere, ozone is a pollutant, but in the stratosphere it filters out harmful ultraviolet radiation.

Ozone Warning – If an ozone warning is issued, it means air quality is poor. People with respiratory issues such as asthma should limit outdoor physical activity.

Pathogen – Any agent that can cause disease.

Precipitation - General name for any water form, falling from clouds.

Radar - An electronic instrument which determines the direction and distance of objects that reflect radio energy back to the radar site. Radar is used to detect hazardous weather.

Rain - Liquid precipitation in the form of water drops that fall from clouds.

Rain Gauge - An instrument used to measure the amount of rain that has fallen. Measurement is done in hundredths of inches (0.01").

Relative Humidity - The ratio of water vapor contained in the air compared to the maximum amount of moisture that the air can hold at that specific temperature and pressure.

Saffir-Simpson Scale - A hurricane intensity scale used to relate hurricane damage to wind speed and central air pressures.

Category 1: wind speeds 74-95 mph
Category 2: wind speeds 96-110 mph
Category 3: wind speeds 111-130 mph
Category 4: wind speeds 131-155 mph
Category 5: wind speeds over 155 mph

The scale also measures the intensity of storm surges (rising sea water levels)

Sandstorm - Strong winds in dry desert regions can carry large amounts sand or dirt through the air. A wall of dirt or sand, sometimes a mile high or wide can resemble a storm as it moves through. They are also referred to as dust storms.

Severe Thunderstorm - Thunderstorms with winds of 58 mph or greater and/or with hail ¾ inch in diameter or larger.

Severe Thunderstorm Warning - Issued when a severe thunderstorm is forecast to occur or is occurring. The warning will include where the storm was occurring, its direction of movement and the primary threat from the storm.

Severe Thunderstorm Watch - Issued when conditions are favorable for the development of severe thunderstorms.

Severe Weather - Any weather event that could possibly be life threatening, or could cause damage.

Showers – Falling rain in scattered areas.

Shear - A variation in wind speed and/or direction.

Sleet - Solid precipitation in the form of ice pellets form when raindrops, originating in warmer air aloft, freeze as they fall through subfreezing air near the surface of the Earth.

Sleet Warning - Issued when accumulations of sleet in excess of a half inch are expected.

Slush - Snow or ice on the ground that has been reduced to a soft, watery mixture by rain or warm temperatures.

Small Craft Advisory - A warning issued by the National Weather Service most frequently in coastal areas. It is issued when winds have reached, or are expected to reach within 12 hours, a speed marginally less than that which is considered gale force, usually 25-38 mph.

Smog - Visible air pollution in urban areas. Smog is formed from smoke and vehicle exhaust.

Snow - Precipitation composed of white ice crystals falling from clouds. Snow is formed when water vapor in the air is less than 32 degrees (F).

Snow Advisory - Issued when snowfall is expected to exceed 2 inches but no more than 5 inches.

Snow Drift – Snow blown by winds that result in increased or uneven accumulations.

Snow Flurries - Brief occurrences of very light snow, producing little or no accumulation.

Snow Showers - Brief occurrences of light or moderate snow, which could produce some light accumulations.

Squall Line - A line of thunderstorms sometimes several hundred miles long that can produce strong thunderstorms and sometimes severe weather.

Stable Air - Air that is colder than its surroundings and is resistant to upward movement.

Stationary Front - A boundary between two air masses that remains stable.

Storm - Any disturbed state of the atmosphere that causes unpleasant weather conditions.

Storm Chaser – A storm chaser is a person who follows tornadoes or other severe weather as a hobby or for research purposes. They often try to get as close as possible to the weather hazard to photograph or document the severity.

Storm Spotter – A person specially trained in the detection, observation and reporting of severe weather. Spotters report information to the National Weather Service so warnings can be issued.

Super Cell - A severe thunderstorm where updrafts and down drafts are in near balance for several hours. Super Cells often produce large hail and tornadoes.

Temperature - The measurement of how hot or cold something is.

Terrorism – The use of unlawful violence or threat of unlawful violence to induce fear; intended to coerce or to intimidate governments or societies in the pursuit of goals that are generally political, religious, or ideological.

Terrorist – A person engaged in the act of terrorism.

Thermometer - An instrument used for measuring temperature.

Thunder - The explosive sound of air expanding as it is heated by lightning.

Tidal Wave – A large wave of water that can cause damage as it comes ashore.

Tornado Warning - Issued when a tornado is expected to occur, or is occurring. The warning will include where the storm was occurring and where it is expected to travel.

Tornado Watch - Issued when conditions are favorable for the development of tornadoes.

Tornado Alley – Area of the central United States where tornadoes occur most frequently.

Tropical Storm - Low pressure disturbances that form in the area over warm tropical ocean waters. Tropical storms typically have winds between 39-73 mph. Tropical storms can progress into hurricanes.

Tropical Depression - Low pressure disturbances that form in the area over warm tropical ocean water. Wind speeds are 38 mph or less. Tropical depressions can progress into tropical storms.

Troposphere - The lowest portion of Earth's atmosphere where weather occurs.

TSA – Abbreviation for the Transportation Security Agency, a federal agency tasked with the protection of US transportation facilities.

Tsunami – A Japanese term for an unusually large ocean wave caused by undersea earthquake, landslide, or volcanic eruption.

Typhoon - A hurricane in the western Pacific Ocean.

Unstable Air - Air that is warmer than its surroundings and tends to rise, leading to the formation of clouds and precipitation.

Virga - Rain or snow that falls from a cloud but evaporates before it reaches the ground.

Visibility - The greatest distance possible for a person to see with their eyes.

Volcano - Any place where lava, ash or volcanic gases escape to the surface of the Earth.

Wall Cloud - Area of clouds that extends underneath a thunderstorm.

Warm Front - The boundary between two air masses, one cool and the other warm, moving so the warmer air replaces the cooler air.

Warning - A forecast issued by the National Weather Service indicating that a specific weather event is actually occurring.

Watch - A forecast issued by the National Weather Service indicating that conditions are favorable for a particular weather hazard.

Waterspout - A tornado occurring over water.

Whiteout – Occurs during extreme blizzard conditions when blowing snow or falling snow reduces visibility so the sky, air, and ground becomes indistinguishable.

Wildfire – A fire in grassy or forested areas that burns out of control. Wildfires can be caused naturally by lightning or by humans, accidentally or intentionally.

WMD – Abbreviation for Weapons of Mass Destruction

Wind – Movement of air relative to the surface of the earth.

Wind Advisory - An advisory from the National Weather Service when winds are expected to be between 29-38 mph, lasting more than one hour, or when wind gusts are expected to be between 44-57 mph.

Wind Chill - The "feel like" temperature when you factor in wind speed with temperature.

Wind Chill Factor - A number that expresses the cooling effect of moving air at different temperatures. Air temperature and wind speed is used in the calculation of wind chill temperatures.

Wind Chill Advisory - Issued when winds of 10 mph or greater are expected to create wind chill factors of 30 degrees below zero or more.

Winter Storm Warning - Issued when hazardous winter weather is occurring. Hazardous winter weather includes heavy snows, blizzards, ice storms, freezing rain, freezing drizzle and sleet.

Winter Storm Watch – A watch is issued when there is a potential for heavy snow or significant ice accumulations, usually at least 24 to 36 hours in advance.

Winter Weather Advisory - The National Weather Service issues these advisories when a low pressure system produces a combination of winter weather (snow, freezing rain, sleet, etc.) that can present a hazard, but does not meet warning criteria.

WX – Abbreviation for weather.

About the Author

Marty Augustine is a veteran law enforcement officer, nationally known safety educator and author. Since 2002, Marty has presented seminars and specialized disaster response training for public safety agencies, the US military, major corporations, and the public. Marty has received numerous awards and recognition for his service to the community.

For more information, visit his website:
www.MartyAugustine.com

He can also be contacted at the address below.

Marty Augustine
P.O. Box 3091
Shawnee, KS 66203

Look for other books by Marty, including "**Storm Safe Kids**", an emergency preparedness guide for children ages 9-12.

Marty's books are available nationwide.

Resources

American Red Cross National Headquarters
2025 E Street, NW
Washington, DC 20006
Website: **www.REDCROSS.org**

Civilian Volunteer Medical Reserve Corps
Office of the Surgeon General
U.S. Department of Health and Human Services
5600 Fishers Lane, Room 18C-14
Rockville, MD 20857
Website: **www.MEDICALRESERVECORPS.gov**

The National Office of Citizen Corps
FEMA Individual and Community Preparedness Div.
Techworld Building, 800 K. Street NW
Suite 640, Washington, D.C. 20472-3630
Website:**www.CITIZENCORPS.gov**

Federal Emergency Management Agency
U.S. Department of Homeland Security
500 C Street SW, Washington, D.C. 20472
Website: **www.FEMA.gov**

National Fire Corps
7852 Walker Drive, Suite 450
Greenbelt, MD 20770
Website: **www.FIRECORPS.org**

Volunteers in Police Service Program
International Association of Chiefs of Police
515 N. Washington St.
Alexandria, VA 22314
Website: **www.POLICEVOLUNTEERS.org**

(All contact information was current at the time of publishing)

Additional Internet Resources

Center for Disease Control
www.CDC.gov

Central Intelligence Agency
www.CIA.gov

Department of Homeland Security
www.DHS.gov

Federal Bureau of Investigation
www.FBI.gov

US Geological Survey
www.USGS.gov

National Oceanic and Atmospheric Administration
www.NOAA.gov

National Security Agency
www.NSA.gov

National Weather Service
www.WEATHER.gov

Transportation Security Administration
www.TSA.gov

National Safety Council
www.NSC.org

This book is not endorsed or supported by any federal agency. Resources are included as references. The author and book have no direct affiliation with any of the agencies listed.

Notes